CORPORATE NETWORKING

Corporate
Networking

Building Channels for Information and Influence

Robert K. Mueller

THE FREE PRESS
A Division of Macmillan, Inc.
NEW YORK

Collier Macmillan Publishers
LONDON

The Free Press
A Division of Macmillan, Inc.
866 Third Avenue, New York, N.Y. 10022

Collier Macmillan Canada, Inc.

Printed in the United States of America

printing number
1 2 3 4 5 6 7 8 9 10

Library of Congress Cataloging-in-Publication Data

Mueller, Robert Kirk.
    Corporate networking.

    1. Communication in management. 2. Information networks. I. Title.
HD30.3.M84   1986   658.4'5   86–18347
ISBN 0–02–922150–1

CONTENTS

Preface   vii

Chapter 1   How to Tap Expert, Unconventional Wisdom: GWRKs   1

Chapter 2   What Is a Network? Something Old, Something New   14

Chapter 3   How and Why Networks Work   28

Chapter 4   Balancing Networks with Hierarchy   41

Chapter 5   The Bureaucratic Bypass   54

Chapter 6   Netcom: Communications Networks, Grapevines, and
              Gossip   72

Chapter 7   The Process of Networking   80

Chapter 8   Hi-Tech Wetenschapswinkels and Hi-Touch Centers   89

Chapter 9   Successfully Managing Innovative Networks   95

Chapter 10   Do I Network? You Can Bet Your Life I Do   106

Chapter 11   *How to Design and Set Up a Network*   *119*

Appendix   *Networkspeak*   *129*

                 Glossary   *133*
                 Notes   *141*
                 Index   *153*

PREFACE

Human networks sink or swim solely on person-to-person linkages. People-power lines represent an organic communications system which can be used to get things done in crises, and in social or opportune situations. Survival of a human or social network depends on mutual, individual trust. Casual, ever-changing connections and friendly, spontaneous ties are often unstable, but they are the informal mechanism at the heart of people networking.

Last November on Veteran's Day my telephone rang early in the morning. The call was from a friend of mine in Purley, Surrey, outside of London. It wasn't that early in Purley, Surrey. My friend's medium-sized British company—a group of electronic and chemical company subsidiaries—was combatting a hostile takeover siege. An unsolicited overture from a New York investment firm had proposed a leveraged buyout (LBO) which would be financed from the United States. My friend's merchant banker, who was also a director of the company as well as a local financial consultant, was unable to readily identify the inquiring principal or his investment firm. Could I help?

My business network worked well on this occasion. That week I was to attend a publisher's advisory board meeting in New York City and a closed-end bond fund board meeting in Springfield, Massachusetts. I could make direct inquiries of several knowledgeable persons about the New York investment firm. Within forty-eight hours I was able to feed back the substance of my network response, albeit a neutral and limited reference check. The "LBO expert" was unknown to three of the largest Wall Street investment banking firms, and only two out of four of the venture capital investment offices contacted in the Boston area had heard anything about the firm. What they had heard was gained in connection with an acquisition in California reportedly arranged by the principal of the LBO expert's company.

Three East Coast consultants contacted came up blank. One was a former consultant with a British merchant banking subsidiary in New York; another was an editor of a New York–based merger and acquisition business journal which specializes in tracking venture capital and LBO activity; the third was a recently retired British industrialist and merchant banker who operates a counseling service out of his New Hampshire home. Contacts with two other fellow board directors who were commercial bank chief executives in Massachusetts also yielded no information. Out of five chief financial officers who served on various boards of directors with me, none had heard of the firm in question or the principal.

Accessing electronic network reports on financial service companies yielded nothing more than an address, the 1982 date of incorporation, and the facts that five employees worked at the firm and the principal was the sole owner. The company's payment practice was slow, but no financial information or other reference data was available. The bottom-line assessment was that the owner in question preferred anonymity, like many of the "nouveau venture capital entrepreneurs," as my Wall Street investment banker friend pejoratively calls them. But that secretiveness is often at the behest of their clients and may not indicate anything regarding the integrity or performance of the firm.

The scene was thus set and my British friend was somewhat better prepared for a face-to-face meeting three weeks later in London when he, his merchant banker, and I received the LBO expert's proposal. While the presentation was an interesting one, my friend eventually pursued the merger route. My personal boardroom network had served its purpose by providing an informal way of accessing people who know enough about what there is to know in order to get something checked, started, or completed.

Not all networking is as successful, but when networks do work the result can come quickly, and the information or action can be effective in solving a problem or assessing a situation.

While a freshman chemical engineer at Washington University in St. Louis I first learned about old boy networks. The experience was a sad and traumatic one, but it taught me a valuable lesson: people networks should not be used unless the empowerment is for a constructive purpose and of mutual advantage to all concerned.

Riding through suburban Brentwood in my blue 1930 Model A roadster, with its socially handy rumble seat, I cruised at twenty miles an hour through a fifteen-mile-an-hour school zone. A traffic ticket ensued. Having just been solemnly inducted into the Missouri Beta chapter of Sigma Phi Epsilon, I first sought comfort at our fraternity house on Kingsbury Street. The influential brother at that time was a silver-haired senior in law school named Mitch, who told me not to worry. He knew the judge in Brentwood and would get my traffic ticket fixed. He assured me that it was no big deal and convinced me to forget the incident.

I did forget it until three weeks later when two police officers extracted me from my parents' home, took me to the police station and proceeded to book me for not appearing in court to answer charges on my traffic violation. This event, understandably, upset my family. It required that my father arrive at midnight to bail me out and pay my fifteen-dollar fine. It was impossible to mention the promise my fraternity brother had made, so, no adequate explanation was available to justify my negligence, much less my driving violation. I've never forgotten the embarrassment that incident caused me nor the lesson on how not to use your networks. Balzac's observation is pertinent here: "Laws are spider webs through which the big flies pass and the little ones get caught." I was caught in my own foolish network expectations.

Networking continued in my early worklife, although I didn't identify it as such then. I was swiftly introduced to the benefits of church, Boy Scout, civil service and ethnic networks. Nevertheless, this introduction did not leave me with an understanding of how certain linkages were activated nor the quid pro quo that made the networking in these organizations work.

During college summer breaks our neighborhood network got me a job as a daytime counselor on one of the toughest playgrounds managed by the City of St. Louis. My Dad was active in the City Missionary Society, along with Conway Briscoe, one of the more prominent civil servants in the city. Our families had known each other from the Shaw Avenue Methodist Church. Mr. Briscoe arranged that, for sixty dollars a week, I join three other college students, also picked because of their families' church connections, as a summer counselor for young Italian children. There were lots of opportunities for these children to get into trouble during the hot, humid weather unless active sports and craft programs were available. This particular city lot was euphemistically called a playground.

It was here that I first learned about gang rape, knife warfare, and the harboring of criminals in the neighboring flats. This was the period of Al Capone, Lucky Luciano, Pretty Boy Floyd, Bonnie and Clyde, and Dillinger, who were in full flower in Chicago, St. Louis, and Kansas City. The Lindbergh kidnapping was also in the news. Despite the police searches and the inquiring newspaper reporters, not even the four- and five-year-old children who were part of this planned recreation program ever peeped about any of the FBI's most-wanted fugitives. I learned later that a fugitive was harbored in the basement of an apartment adjoining the playground. The ethnic network was tightly controlled and most effective.

Our family contacts and neighborhood friends helped me land my first full-time job upon my graduation from college. It was at Sinclair Oil Company's refinery in East Chicago, Illinois, back before Sinclair followed its dinosaur advertising image into oblivion. This was in 1935 when jobs were hard to find at $1.25 an hour on the night shift and climbing the ladder in an oil company required either a geology major or a more specialized education. I ran viscosity tests for control purposes in operating the refinery. Our neighbor, Guy Brown, was a City of St. Louis head of the Civil Engineering Department and active with my Dad on Boy Scout Troop 245 in Lindenwood. Mrs. Anne Brown had gone to school with Harry Sinclair who was responsive when she called him to get a freshly minted chemical engineer, me, into his company. I never met the legendary Harry but was grateful for the family Boy Scout network that got me into the fume-laden East Chicago refinery environment.

When an opening on the 12:00–8:00 A.M. shift at the Queeny Plant of Monsanto in St. Louis became available, I opted for running analytical tests on saccharine in order to pursue my first love of chemistry. Taking this new job also saved me money because I could live at home with my parents. I was back in the neighborhood, church, and old school networks I had established while at Washington University.

Chapter 1

How to Tap Expert, Unconventional Wisdom: GWRKs

> . . . and they that weave networks, shall be confounded.
> —*Isaiah, XIX, 9*

Organization as we know it is obsolete in the information society in which we now exist. Those of us in management who weave human networks have confounded both ourselves and our establishments. These human networks are thriving while the organizations around them struggle to be effective—or even to survive. There seems to be an intuitive notion that somehow, someway, networking may be basic to organizing and managing people in the future.

The challenge is to create a proper dynamic balance in the management and control of our organizational system. This balancing requires the fostering of the human, innovative side of business systems management, which is where networks and networking play a key role.

In dealing with such a challenge, we are presented with a choice between the management of human systems and human systems management. The management of human systems is the science and technology of managing productivity and efficiency. Institutionalization, hierarchical structures, orderly processes, and bureaucracy abound. Human systems management is the art of linking human beings in constructive teams and catalyzing their full creative growth through leadership. Innovation, entrepreneurship, risk taking, networking, motivation, communication, recognition, individualism,

1

self-fulfillment, strong peer relationships, and professional dedication are key attributes of this type of management.

This book argues that the concept of human networks and the process of social networking are prime components for a properly balanced organizational system in these turbulent and exciting times. Formal recognition and use of human networks is limited and somewhat unacceptable in the traditional hierarchical and structured makeup of most of our institutions. However, the good news is that networks and networking can cohabit with hierarchy and bureaucracy. Effectiveness and action-timing can often be enhanced with proper empowerment of the human networks which already exist in all organizations. One way to get things done quicker and better, given the barriers and complexities in our political, economic, educational, social, and technological institutions, is to "think networks," i.e., identify and encourage them where appropriate.

This proposed networking mind-set is alien to most executives and managers. They got where they are by climbing the ladder of traditional, hierarchical, organizational pyramids. The Orwellian mentality, which is so often the result of this process, needs to be blended with a Renaissance mentality to enable managers to recognize the value of new strains of organization such as human networks. Classical institutional structures, processes, and concepts have failed to keep up with the demands for survival, interdependence, growth, and improved effectiveness of many of our organizations. Networks and networking warrant special attention from leaders and managers for the future.

THE HEART OF NETWORKING: BLEST BE WEAK TIES THAT BIND

Networks and networking flourish in the domain of the social and behavioral scientists. Few of us in management or administrative positions are trained or educated in such hi-touch, soft-science professions. Even fewer of us have the courage to explore these misty fields in a business organization or economic context because hi-touch expertise in management is often unrewarded.

As far as the professional experts in these matters are concerned, one claims, "We often spend so much time analyzing the stem, stamen, pistil, and petal that we do not see the flower." The floral metaphor is appropriate. Networking is like trying to cultivate wildflowers. You don't plant and hover over them. You permit or create an environment where they can come out and grow.

Many large corporate organizations are experiencing a disruption of traditional structures and management information processes. Their efforts to keep up with people needs, value shifts, and exploding networks have been in vain. Networks and networking, like wildflowers, spring up in such an atmosphere of transformation in big institutions. Let's hypothesize about the characteristics of this "confounded" networking process and specific networks; maybe by doing so we can empower the networking to continue.

Networks are needs-driven and deliberate. Some of them are even sanctioned. Tandem Computer Inc., in Cupertino, California, is a computer hardware manufacturer with a $624 million turnover and a reputation for its enlightened management culture. The company produces "fail-safe system" computers for banking, defense, and telecommunications. Fourteen of the world's major stock exchanges run on Tandem's computers. It is understandable then why Tandem's president and chief executive, Jim Treybig, provides each employee with a personal computer and why, after an employee has worked at Tandem for six months, the computer becomes his or her personal property.

The company functions effectively and routinely with most everyone hooked up electronically to one another to carry out the conventional administrative and engineering tasks. Cathode ray tube (CRT) dialoging is encouraged and practiced in conducting daily business affairs. One goes direct, via his or her computer hookup, to the person who can get something done. The normal hierarchy and bureaucracy are bypassed.

So much for Tandem's fluid, floppy disc and family-style management communications practice. Many progressive companies have jumped on this computerized management bandwagon. It's fashionable and fun, as well as efficient. However, the "new" confounding twist is human networking beyond the computer, going back to behavioral basics. Politicians call it "pressing the flesh." The term refers to one-to-one relationships. Jim Treybig is a keen radio ham who spends his holidays bouncing radio signals off the moon. Treybig believes, above all, in communication between all levels of his workforce worldwide—by computer, films, and television. Tandem supplements its electronic networking with a free beer and pretzel party at each plant every Friday night. All employees are invited to gather at the end of a computer-dominated week of work to engage in human networking and chat about the business. The management doesn't label these informal happenings as human network-shops. But that is precisely what they are. These optional meetings are fun-and-game times. They are vital ceremonies or rituals that have more than symbolic significance in their informality.

These parties serve four major functions. They provide an opportunity to socialize, allay anxieties, reduce ambiguities and convey the message that the company cares and values its employees.

Mary Kay Cosmetics, Inc., uses similar human networking events as a frame of reference for conducting its business. When 7,000 women gather at the annual seminar, they come to hear messages from Mary Kay, applaud achievements of star salespeople, hear success stories, and celebrate symbols of their corporate culture. The networks and networking are empowered by such ritualistic occasions.

A New York–based multinational company conducts its consumer product businesses with similar attention to the value of human networking. Because the headquarters delegates primary management functions to separate company units around the globe (which are free to use their own style), communicating between locations can be a problem. But the management's networking skills are way beyond those of the typical holding company with a decentralized business control structure. People-to-people relations are vital with the creative, entrepreneurial talent in the organization.

The annual conference of managing directors and general managers with the top executives of this company is a social-business happening. It is held—rather elaborately staged with whistles and bells—at various impressive locations around the world to take advantage of the company's international nature. A week of breezy business reviews, new product revelations and planning discussions, and entertainment by professional actors constitutes the formalized program. Joe, the executive vice president, is a dynamic person who makes it clear that a major benefit of the meeting event is the human networking phase when he busily works the crowd of 150 managers, researchers, inventors, and artists. It ranks equally in importance to the formal agenda.

Business discussions and product presentations are interspersed with social and recreational programs. This encourages personal exchanges between managers located in New Zealand and Massachusetts, Mexico City and Amsterdam, and so on. I had the privilege of being with this imaginative group in Montreux, Switzerland, in June

1984, and observed the interchange of human networks in the Swiss Riviera, Gstaad, and Gruyère, where some of the extracurricular activities took place.

This is an innovative and creative group of professional managers who, because their business is so humanistically oriented, network easily among themselves. Human networking is considered a generic process which supplements the professional business administration skills that are obviously necessary to run a profitable enterprise.

A manager's dilemma is how to maintain control while allowing enough slack to create an atmosphere conducive to innovation. This balance depends on networks and networking as much as it does on conventional business administration skills. Unless the phenomenon of networking is understood there may not be enough loyalty to and respect for the management system nor enough new ideas for the next product introduction.

Generally, networks are tacitly tolerated in even the most rigid organizations. However, because networks are semiprivate, partly hidden relationships, they change their nature when they are exposed. Like grapevines and rumor mills, networks are capable of reprisals if unacceptably tinkered with.

I remember the imposition of a policy having to do with airline travel credits in a company I worked with several years ago. This was in the early days of earning bonus mileage on an airline by frequent use of its services. The practice of "pocketing" these bonus mileage slips earned on company business flights to build up enough for a personal airline trip was quietly tolerated by managers without any formal policy declaration by the company.

The accountants didn't do much traveling so it was some time before they became aware that bonus mileage credits earned on company business flights were being kept for personal use. When this networking practice was found out by a zealous accountant, it was like the Watergate break-in discovery. Stilted memos went out to all staff, pointing out that these bonus credits were property of the company since they were earned on business trips. The bonus mileage was to be turned into the company to be used "legitimately" on other business travel.

The staff rebelled, not in a clamorous way but by posting a series of anonymous notes on bulletin boards. There began an undercover circulation of satirical, fake memos addressed ostensibly by the management to all employees. I remember one particular pseudo memo which was circulated worldwide in a matter of a week. It went into great detail on the rationale behind the "official" yellow sheet announcement. The memo stated that since business trips were on company time and at company expense, any rebate in the form of bonus mileage granted by the airline was company property and belonged to the clients, customers, and shareholders. Given this logic, all employees were instructed to return to the company any airline slippers, mini-toiletry kits, macadamia nuts, or other amenities handed out by cabin attendants on business flights. The official company policy was ridiculed to such an extent that it had to be rescinded. Management had paid the price for tampering with a small but highly personal perquisite enjoyed by the travel-weary staff.

These networks of understanding (or misunderstanding) spring up in almost every organization. They can exist in the form of an overlay to what is spelled out in conventional policy manuals as acceptable working practices. Or they can exist as an underlay to private communication contacts. Accordingly, a network is not a thing, it is a process.

NOURISHING NETWORKS

If networks do exist in most every human organization, healthy networking must contribute in some way to healthy institutional cultures. This poses an interesting hypothesis: networking may be a necessary prelude to setting up a formal organization. If this is the case, let us examine how to create environments which are conducive to constructive networking.

Since networks and networking are everywhere and "everybody does it," the normality of networks needs to be recognized by potential managers. Many companies do try to nourish networks without identifying their actions as such. The cultivation of employee clubs, sports and social events, credit unions, and other service groups is an example of how management can encourage personal interaction, and a sense of achievement and satisfaction among employees.

One company, Arthur D. Little, Inc. (ADL), a contract research and consulting firm in Cambridge, Massachusetts, nourishes employee networking at Christmastime by including in its corporate budget extra funds which are distributed to all organizational units on a dollars-per-capita basis. These optional funds are spend during the holiday season and are intended for human networking purposes, usually a social event. Each unit makes up its own party guest list and invites only those, from inside or outside the corporation, that fit their urge to network. Top management may or may not be included. The location of the social event is either in a series of gathering rooms at the company's offices or in the private home of a staff member.

This light touch of network nourishment at year's end recognizes the highly personal qualities of networking. Overorganizing these holiday social events would cause them to fall apart. The injection of official monitoring or structuring of the unofficial personal relationships that are so valuable in setting the climate of the organization would destroy the networking process. There is no manipulation or coercion in any form, only resource allocation.

Having participated by personal invitation (rather than by any requirement that the senior management are, exofficio, included in all parties) in many of these events, I can attest to the extent that human networking takes place—even before the wassail bowl is empty. Company and personal information is exchanged naturally and in a relaxed manner. The negative aspects of employee griping and criticism of company actions or inactions are more than offset by the positive feelings. The gaps between power and authority, between senior and junior members of the organization, between support and professional staff, are narrowed by these networking events.

GWRKs

> If the word and concept of networks have become fashionable, it is not a sign of whim and fancy but a recognition of the brute fact of *limited* resources and *limitless* problems.[1]
> —Seymour B. Sarason, Professor of Psychology,
> Yale University

Networks love truth no matter how bad it is, according to Bryon Kennard, National Chairman of Earth Day 1980, author and social critic. And the way to get at the truth is to ask the person who *really* knows what he or she is talking about. You can't expect to know everything. So, what's important is to know where to go to find out what you must know before you need to know it.

My friend, W. Alec Jordan, founding editor of *Chemical Week,* has for years maintained a special guys-who-really-know (GWRK) file in his office.[2] This secret file is a reference list of Alec's friends on whom he can rely and whose knowledgeability he reveres.

I have a similar file at home and at the office, but it includes both guys and gals who really know. Alec is in my card index, not as a riposte to my being in his GWRK file but because he is an expert on the chemical industry and an unconventional thinking about the way people behave. He and I have shared opinions, contacts, and fun through the years. We enjoy irregular networking with each other on the damndest topics—higher education, corporate governance, and chemical industry mores and foibles.

As individuals we all act either as nodes or links in various networks. Some of us function as both. A node in a network is the recipient of resources or information. Alec and I are nodes in our respective networks. In contrast, links serve as conveyors of information and connect those who have information with those who need it. They can be people or other sources of information such as this book, a newsletter, or a computer data base.

According to Leif Smith and Pat Wagner of the Denver-based Network Resources, Inc., some people function as "weavers." They know about many of the nodes and links in various networks. They move about, figuratively speaking, within the networks bringing together any person who needs to be connected with another person. In the case of weavers, networking is a business.

My experience with those persons interested in networks and networking is that they are able to finger experts and unconventional thinkers. There is a fascinating myriad of loosely organized networks out there to tap into when you need information or expert help. Networks are quest facilitators in an open system with a changing information base. Pat Wagner says only 5 percent of her data base is on computers. The 95 percent remaining is instinct, social experience, know how, and know who.

One day last year I was struggling with an overseas client's problem on how to create an atmosphere conducive to innovation in a multinational corporation in the consumer products business. That particular industry is dominated by the dynamics of fashion and fad. There is an unpredictable market response to the many new products which flood the distributors each season. Who could have predicted the success of video games, Cabbage Patch dolls, Silly Putty, *Star Wars*, or Care Bears?

The problem I faced was finding expert opinion on how to keep the fires of innovation and creativity alive while maintaining business control. My personal network—my GWRK file—came in handy. In 1969 I had chaired a three-week seminar on innovation and the management of technology at the Schloss Leopoldskron in Salzburg, Austria. Even after fifteen years I was able to tap into the resources of experts from the seminar through their writing. Ideas on innovation offered by faculty members of Stanford, Dartmouth, Columbia, and the University of Michigan were valuable to my presentation. The information from these sources was matched with some 1984 case studies of innovative companies, such as, 3M, Apple Computer, Merrill-Lynch, Bank of America, Medtronics, Schlage, American Express, and others who cooperated in a study on corporate innovativeness conducted by ADL.

Information was also gathered from a check on the innovation management practices of companies in North America, Europe, and Japan. And, the personal opinions I gathered from my own network contacts were supplemented by a survey of 5,828 questionnaires given to executives around the world.

The primary findings from the survey were: (1) top management is becoming more dependent on innovation as a means to generate profit and growth; (2) North American companies are less likely to have specific corporate expectations for the contribution of innovation; (3) innovation can be managed but it requires specific skills and knowledge; (4) CEOs vary in their assessment of their roles in innovation; (5) several barriers must be overcome if companies are to become more innovative; (6) there are three phases to innovation—invention, incubation, and introduction; (7) creating a favorable climate is the most important single factor in encouraging innovation; (8) the sources of inspiration vary across cultures; (9) Japanese executives take a broader view of innovation; (10) new organizational mechanisms are being used to overcome traditional barriers; and (11) the creative use of compensation systems and other rewards can reinforce innovation.

Networks are used to improve communications. They increase awareness, morale, and needs-gratification. Networks help individuals, project teams, family units, and task forces to expand their boundaries. An example of this is when lonely hearts clubs set up pen pal relationships between two people. Sometimes these relationships flower into something more exciting and rewarding. The requirements for extending boundaries include learning how to access elusive networks and how to stimulate network formation and empowerment.

This learning has to take place despite and in terms of environmental conditions of an organization. The formal, conventionally structured company does not usually recognize networks in any explicit way. The federal government's byzantine agency and bureaucratic maze is perhaps an extreme example of the limitations of hierarchy and traditional institutional geometry. The reason the lobby phenomenon has grown so much is that it is the only way to get anything done in Washington, D.C. The methods of functioning of the 6,500 lobbyists registered in the nation's capital are primarily networking and networks. The political process is not violated by the existence of these networks but, rather, facilitated by the direct contact and communication networks which are woven into the hierarchy and bureaucracy inherent in the federal government's structural setup.

Let us reflect on the purposes of networking. Power is a prime driving force:

- Networkers can accumulate influence or power by gathering and controlling information unavailable to them in hierarchical situations.

- Common interests, ideology, or social position can build a power base.

- Personal chemistry, friendship, and peer relationships are powerful forces in human situations.

- Adequate communication between people is the result of the connecting power of of networks.

- Networks can be viewed as promoters of culture. Norms, values, beliefs, and codes are transmitted by networks.

- Networking can be considered a necessary prelude to the establishment of a organization. Once a formal structure is created the network disappears unless the leaders make special arrangements to preserve these subtle connections. Smart managers leave networks alone as much as possible and consider them invaluable to the formal organization structure.

A CHEMICAL NETWORK OF EXPERTS

Another example of a GWRK expert network is the Chemical Estate which is part of the ADL worldwide organization of over 1,500 professionals. In 1983 ADL formed a Chemical Council with 13 members of its staff. The council's project was to identify and register 300 professionals in the ADL organization who had formal chemical education and experience. The council was established because the parent organization needed to be able to effectively reach the GWRKs—those on the staff who really know the global chemical domain and its scientific, technological, industrial, and economic dynamics.

The story of the formation of this network—dubbed ADL's Chemical Estate Network—is based on symbolism of the chemical profession, function, and some classical tenets of networking theory as applied to a contract research and consulting practice. It has proven to be a good model for tapping the unconventional wisdom of GWRKs in the chemical world. The ADL Chemical Registry identifies:

- 300 professionals worldwide
  in 15 overlapping nets of affinity "tribal" groups of professional staff (units, sections, subsidiaries, and offices)
  with 177 nodes of expertise in the areas of chemical and related products, processes, and technology

- 15 autonomous (floating) segments which are organizationally self-sufficient

- No single paramount leader controls or speaks for the network.

How does this network of chemical experts really function to get things done in a more effective manner than other organizations of qualified professionals in various chemically related fields? Three examples illustrate the networking process.

First, at monthly meetings Chemical Council members representing most all the various chemically related units and sections of the professional staff meet for a working lunch. Each attendee has about five minutes to informally tell the group what is going on in his or her area of interest and activity. This round-robin exchange reveals new business and technology trends, future prospects, new staff recruits, requests for collaboration from other council members, and any professional opinions thought to be of possible interest to the worldwide chemical estate.

These monthly meetings have, for example, speeded the linkage of qualified technical support from the United States to the United Kingdom to help achieve a restructuring of the Turkish fertilizer industry; spread the "innovation gospel" and practice of using an original opinion survey instrument—"The Innovation Climate Index"—developed by the ADL San Francisco office to assess barriers to innovation in a Scandinavian-based chemical conglomerate. Chemically oriented staff members of ADL's Brussels office were assigned to the client problem in a coastal industrial complex in Sweden as the result of an exchange between Chemical Council members.

Second, the crisis atmosphere created worldwide in the chemical industry in December 1984 when the Bhopal tragedy occurred in India provided an occasion for the Chemical Council network to quickly organize a response to those directly concerned with acute and chronic industrial accidents and exposure potential. A special Chemical Council meeting was called and a program developed to offer help to companies and organizations concerned with short- and long-term remedial and protective actions. The program included an updating of a 1983 accident history of various companies around the world in industrial sectors such as pesticides, synfuels, refineries, explosives, metals, rubber production, petrochemicals, and fertilizers. These accidents were classified by geography, prominent material categories, acute or chronic hazard implications, and frequency and severity of incident.

An invitational seminar—"Rethinking Risk Management: A New Agenda"—was arranged for early February 1985 in the greater New York area with eight speakers from ADL's London and Cambridge, Massachusetts staffs, plus three chemical company executives and consultants from Europe and the United States. The key environmental safety officer from Union Carbide presented a technical report of the methyl isocyanate release in India. The discussion among the eighty-five guests proved to be an enlightening event of assistance to the industry and an opportunity to offer outside perspectives and consulting resources to the participants. The business results of this and subsequent professional activity were significant as public and industry concern continued to mount during 1985.

A third example of the Chemical Council's networking process was the rapid development of a proposed model chemical plant of the future, devised by the professional staff in the chemical, metallurgical, and nuclear engineering sections ADL. The proposal suggested significant changes in chemical plant design, including hazardless-specific layouts, third-party audits, accrual funds for contingent use, improved engineering drills, advance maintenance management, closed loop control systems, and many safety features which are common in the nuclear utility industry but not traditionally used in chemical industry plant design.

The value and effectiveness of identifying and empowering human networks to supplement any traditional organizational structure or management process depends on several initiatives: understanding the nature or heart of networks, nourishing them appropriately, finding the GWRKs, and taking collegial action as demonstrated by the Chemical Council's successful experiences.

If we don't transform our conventional, hierarchical structures into cross-level networking systems, many of our institutions will continue to decrease in effectiveness. Because sophisticated information retrieval capabilities and social networking are undercutting and perturbing the neatly charted, pyramidal structures of conventional institutions, it has become necessary for companies to acknowledge the value of social and communications networks and networking. While a networking organization will be more complex and have administrative supervision unrelated to technological or business direction, the networking overlay (or underlay) will provide an enormous information base that is readily available and useful. Anyone will be able to go to anyone else swiftly and directly . . . to the guys and gals who really know.

Chapter 2

What Is a Network? Something Old, Something New

> *Networks*: ensnaring, entanglement; the attribute and property of all gods who bind and the ensnaring, negative aspect of the feminine power, the Great Mother, who is often a goddess of nets. Network is symbolic of a complex relationship beyond the mere time-space sequence, unlimited relationship; a structure formed of the visible and the invisible; it is also unity.
> —*J. C. Cooper[1]*

FROM THE SUBLIME TO THE RETICULIST

Much earlier in time, Dr. Samuel Johnson, the renowned British lexicographer, topped Mr. Cooper's lofty definition, albeit even more opaquely. He called a network "anything reticulated and decussated at equal distances with interstices at the intersections"! *Reticular* means being like a net in operation or effect. Some social scientists use the fancy term *reticulist* for those who have networking skills, i.e., a networker. This language adds undue complication to the very simple notion of a human network as a person-to-person connection, affinity, or relationship.

Behavioral scientists get in the act with their own vocabulary. Networks are termed "loosely organized systems" (LOS) and defined as those systems where there are personal attachments. An LOS tends to be "circumscribed, infrequent, weak in its mutual effects, unimportant and/or slow to respond," according to K. S. Weick.[2] It often lacks clear boundaries. Membership in the system can be unimportant and not at all salient for the unit's own members. In an LOS, the degree of functional interdependence is low.

Ordinarily, people are tied together in organizations because the requirements of their roles are interrelated. Most systems are "tightly organized systems" (TOS) such as a manufacturing company. Any weak links at critical points of interdependence are cause for management concern. In an LOS, on the other hand, there are fewer strong connections between the networkers than there are normally in a highly structured organization. In most of our institutions, hierarchy and bureaucracy are intrinsic. In networks, the connections are lateral. Actually, they can be up, down, or sideways. They can even be linkages via a third party, i.e., indirect contacts or relationships.

NETWORKS ARE ANOTHER WORLD

Lipnack and Stamps have done an impressive and scholarly task of gathering information on human networking as it has existed throughout the history of mankind.[3] The literature on networks has been described as a terminological jungle in which any newcomers may plant a tree. Lipnack and Stamps' book is an excellent place to begin to explore this forest of resources and ideas about networking of the nontennis, nonelectronic kind.

Networks on a small scale, in families, tribes, clans, neighborhoods, schools, churches, and most local social settings, are commonly acknowledged. Further, they are well known for their relevance to person-to-person relationships. Primitive societies were primarily family networks organized in tribal form. The tribal leader was at the helm, the center of this closely networked organization. His power and influence radiated out in a spiderweb form through his family, relatives, and associates. Those in closest contact with the "spider" or tribal chief wielded the most influence. As the lines of power got more distant from the center of the tribe they were reduced in importance.

The advantages of this tribal power network are strong leadership, speedy decision making, and trust in the leader. Tribal cultures and network models that have had to adapt to contemporary circumstances fall short on record keeping and control. Crony networking emerges. The network becomes elitist. The individual is subordinate to the organization.

While the tribal network model exists in many small firms or sectors of larger companies, it has its limitations in meshing with hierarchy and other structural features of bureaucratic organizations. If the positive features of a tribal network can be nested within a sector of a large organization, the organization can reap the benefits of the strong power and influence of a club network.

Modern managers need to understand the power and limitations of a tribal network and adjust the managerial mind-set to acknowledge this original network culture which could get things done when existence was less complex. There are times when a tribal network culture is most effective—even in these complicated times: remote, overseas office organizations, start-up teams, specialized functional groups such as audit teams, quality control departments, partnerships, emergency organizations, and problem-solving task forces. With a strong leader, an organization with a tribal network can be very effective.

Networks in a physical sense are also well recognized in communications systems (telephone, radio, TV, computers), information services (publications, libraries, stock market quotations), electronic devices and systems, and transportation systems (railways, airways, waterways, highways). These are engineering and technology network examples.

Silicon Valley is perhaps one of the best examples of the profound transformation in our nation's networking habits. With the focus on the electronics and telecommunications industry, it is not unexpected that the information flow is open and constant in this region of Northern California. Networking is the mode of communication. The authors of *Silicon Valley Fever*, Everett Rogers and Judith Larsen, characterize Silicon Valley "not as just a geographical area but as a network."[4]

Exchange and movement of key personnel is frequent here. There is so much going on that information has to be shared between technologists as the state of the art advances rapidly. In 1985 Silicon Valley went through a slowdown due to economic and competitive forces, but the survivors continued to network feverishly despite the employment uncertainties.

The human or social networks are older than the physical system networks. Strangely, less is known about their nature, even though networking on an individual, personalized basis and in small organizations is part of our daily lives.

One of my favorite playwrights, London's Alan Ayckbourn, based his twenty-eighth play, *Intimate Exchanges*, on the various chains of events which follow from relatively trivial decisions made by a British woman in a family situation. The action takes place for the most part in and around Bilbury Lodge, a preparatory school for boys and girls. The woman's initial decision is whether to have the first cigarette of the day before 6:00 P.M. On some nights she can resist having one; on others she can't.

The two, quite separate chains of events that result from this initial decision lead to another character making two more decisions, and so on, as events spread out into a web of social drama and intrigue. The network of human interactions reaches the lives of a host of individuals who have the "intimate exchanges."

Two actors, Lavina Bertram and Robert Herford, played multiple adult parts in different versions produced at the Ambassadors Theatre on West Street, off Shaftesbury Theatre street in downtown London. Ten of the sixteen versions were presented in the 1984–1985 theater season. (See fig. 2.1.)

Intimate Exchanges is a theatrical and revealing account of networks and networking on a personalized level as they exist in everyday living. No analysis, no theories, no sociological vocabulary, and no sermons are involved. Yet the process by which the characters' relationships are woven in and out of marriage, careers, school, religion, leisure, retirement, rites of birth and death, rituals of love, hate and conflict, presents the human condition as an intricate, sensitive, and interconnected web of personal networks that make our world go around. The plays are worth seeing for the delightful, funny entertainment they provide alone, but they are also worth seeing for the way in which they subtley illustrate the theme of how things get done by human networks and networking.

We don't particularly need a theory to identify and empower our own friendship networks. But there are sociologists and anthropologists who have provided enlightening perspectives on the characteristics of people's network relationships and the processes involved. (See Chapter 3 for one network model, a structural theory of action.)

From an individual standpoint there are two models of network relationships: one is based on personal friendships, acquaintanceships and connections, and another is based on structural, occupational

intimate exchanges

At the very start of *Intimate Exchanges,* a woman is faced with a small, fairly trivial decision. Should she resist having the first cigarette of the day before 6.00pm?
On some nights, her willpower is strong enough; on others it isn't.

The two quite separate chains of events that result from her choice lead, by the end of scene one, to another character making two further decisions, this time of a slightly more important nature. Just before the interval two more choices, more crucial still, are to be made. Finally preceding the fourth and final scene, another two major courses of action remain to be chosen by the characters.
What you will see tonight, then, is a single strand of a much larger web of interconnecting alternative scenes. Each evening is intended to be complete in itself although it will, of course, be only ever one version of what might have happened if . . .
I hope curiosity will bring you back to see some of the other 'ifs'. There are sixteen versions, though in this season we are presenting ten, some vastly different; some only slightly so. If you're in any doubt – the display board in the foyer will tell you what particular strand you'll be seeing or have seen tonight. I particularly wish to thank the brave and remarkable cast of two for agreeing to take part in this piece of theatrical lunacy.

Alan Ayckbourn

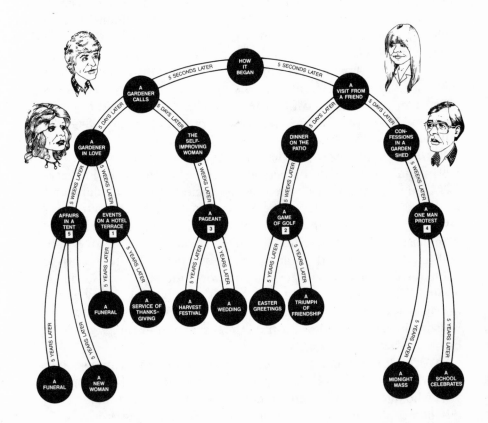

——————— PERFORMANCE SCHEDULE ———————

1. EVENTS ON A HOTEL TERRACE . . . . .29th OCT – 17th NOV
2. A GAME OF GOLF . . . . .19th NOV – 8th DEC
3. A PAGEANT . . . . .10th DEC – 5th JAN
4. A ONE MAN PROTEST . . . . .7th JAN – 26th JAN
5. AFFAIRS IN A TENT . . . . .28th JAN – 16th FEB

FIGURE 2.1: *Intimate Exchanges,* a play about personal networks.
(Reproduced with permission of Alan Ayckbourn.)

positions in one or more network systems such as a job in a corporation, government office, school or hospital, or a role in a social club
or association. The first model deals with "ego networks" and the
second with "network position."

The ego network is also called primary star, primary zone, first
order zone, or personal network. Models of ego networks have been
developed most extensively by anthropologists who extend sociometry studies in order to conduct empirical research on large populations.[5] An ego network is usually measured by the extent to which it
provides support for the people in it. Ego networks are "dense,"
meaning that all involved are connected by intense relationships with
each other.

Ego networks attend to the relations in which a person is involved. They may miss the potential importance of his or her lack of
relations with other significant status occupants in the system. Ego
networks only involve the individual's direct relations to others and
may omit or be oblivious of unreciprocated relations with some persons who have no direct relationship, but may have an indirect connection. Saying this more simply, if we confine our networking to
only those whom we know personally (or positionally), we miss the
"other world" out there of contacts and friends of our contacts and
friends. This is the exciting, potential scope which networking offers
when conducted in a conscious and determined way.

Personal obligation networks are an offshoot of ego networks. In
the business world you can only use your personal collateral in a limited way in getting appointments or seeking special attention. This is
a reciprocal exchange that can be shared from time to time with those
with whom you have connections on a transaction or business basis
(as distinct from a superior-subordinate relationship).

As the studies of cultural anthropologists show, such personal obligation networks are as old as the hills and exist all over the world. A
recent study done in Mexico and Turkey illustrates this point. Due to
the caste system, the Maya of Zinacantan, a township in Chiapas,
Mexico, are economically restricted from advancing in the society in
general. They, therefore, seek advancement within their villages
through what are generally known as "personal obligation networks" rather than by any direct accumulation of wealth. These personal obligation networks are most often found through kinship networks related to inheritances, bridewealth, and employment within
the family. They are similar to the informal networks found in Ankara, Turkey, wherein migrants maintain networks within their vil-

lages as support systems for themselves and as an informal welfare system for newly arriving migrants.

The network position model describes a person's relationships with all other people in a system—an organization, for example. It differs from an ego network principally because the relationships one does not have to others in the system are as important as the relationships one does have.

Two other models have been used extensively by sociologists to describe socially integrated people: position centrality and position prestige. Models of *position centrality* in a network stem from the analyses of communications networks by Bavelas[6] and Leavitt.[7] A person's position in a network is central to the extent that all relationships in the network involve him or her. Models of *position prestige* in a network stem from an analysis of popularity: to what extent does a person have strong relationships with influential members in the network?

All of these positional and ego relationships tend to foster network cliques. A clique is a set of people in a network who are connected to one another by strong relationships. Examples of cliques are family, playgroup, community, and friendship networks. These groups of people are characterized by having intimate face-to-face association and cooperation.

There are two challenges involved in the networking process. The *first* is to nurture and empower our ego model and position model networks. The *second* is to extend these networks to "another world" beyond our ken. This is where a theory of networking is useful. To be able and willing to use networking in large organizations, going beyond the traditional, personal acquaintance networks, offers a chance to improve organizational effectiveness.

THE NATURE OF NETWORKS AND NETWORKING

The recent writings of Lipnack and Stamps, Ferguson,[8] Henderson,[9] and others have added to the seminal work of former University of Florida social anthropologist Virginia Hine, who is best known, along with Luther Gerlach of the University of Minnesota, as the creator of the network theory of sociocultural interaction.[10] The concept of "another America," or an "aquarian society" represents a subtle but powerful subcultural set of social transformation movements, not only in America but throughout the world. As Lipnack and Stamps characterize it: "another America" is "pulsating, expanding, and unfolding through networking, an organic communications process that threads across interests, through problems, and around solutions. Networks are the meeting grounds for the inhabitants of this invisible domain. These flexible, vibrant organizations often exist without boundaries, bylaws, or officers. Networks are the lines of communications, the alternative express highways that people use to get things done. In crisis and in opportunity, the word spreads quickly through these people-power lines."[11]

Networks, according to the various experts, are informal systems where dissonance is encouraged and consensus a common goal. The nature of networks is that they are short-lived, self-camouflaging, and adisciplinary. They represent crosshatches of activity in constantly changing form. Networks are invisible, uncountable, unpollable, and may be active or inactive.[12] In practical terms, networks feature spontaneous feedback via telephone, mail, meetings, computers, or a shout across the room, if this is possible.

Hierarchical structures are essentially taboo in human networks as far as concept, power, and influence are concerned. The Great Atlantic Radio Conspiracy of Baltimore, Maryland, is a network of the airways. It is a collective that produces and distributes award-winning, broadcast-quality audiotapes on politics, protests, the media, the arts, liberation struggles abroad, women, men, radicalism, professions, holidays, food, health, etc. "We have no leader," the collective states. "We are all workers in an anti-hierarchical society."

Network *structures* have one or more of five characteristics according to the Lipnack and Stamps representation[13]:

1. "Wholeparts"—self-reliant and autonomous participants, i.e., independent "wholes" and interdependent "parts"

2. Levels—the result of networks interconnecting on an ever-expanding scale

3. Distributed powers and responsibility along horizontal or wavy lines (*not* the rigid, vertical lines found in bureaucracies)

4. Fly-eyed perception—having one apparent eye or focus that embodies a plethora of other eyes

5. Hydra-headed direction—having many "leaders" (polycephalous) yet few rings of power

Network *processes* have one or more of five characteristics:

1. Relationships—abstract and qualitative as well as concrete and quantitative

2. Fuzziness—having few inner divisions and indistinct borderlines

3. Nodes and links—serving as entry points or connectors for conveying information

4. "Me" and "we" relationships—according equal importance to the individual and the group

5. Values—self-reliance, self-interest, interdependence, and collective-interest

An interesting example of corporate networking, using the structures and processes outlined, is the work of the Atlanta-based Network Builders International (NBI). This company uses hi-tech innovation to restore the sense of cooperation and trust common to small communities a century ago.

NBI is a training and consulting firm that creates a computerized networking directory to serve as a "handbook of hidden resources" for persons willing to share knowledge, experience, and skills. Individuals use the directory like the *Yellow Pages*, accessing relevant information according to their interests. Hour-long, information-gathering workshops with participants who are members of an organization typically yield about 4,000 entries from an organizational group of, say, 100 people. The entries are placed in 14 categories which range from skills, hobbies, travel, and games to health, support groups, and family relationships. The information is compiled, processed through a computerized software system and distributed to each member.

NBI noted that the directory increases educational cooperation among members. For instance, parents with child-rearing problems or persons with diet problems choose to communicate with others having similar interests.

NBI has helped launch metropolitan learning networks in Chicago and Atlanta, and it is active in Seattle, San Francisco, and Los Angeles. One directory now has a 14-category statistical breakdown of how 70,000 people in metropolitan networks use information. The handbook is a multidimensional communication tool that aids in problem solving and community building.

THE HIDDEN SOCIAL CONTRACTS

Human networks and networking abide by implicit social contracts between persons who extend the terms of these informal contracts beyond their own ego and positional network boundaries. If you as a network member don't like the social contract, you have the option of creating a social contract network that suits your taste.

To understand the full import of this freedom of choice in human relations, we need to understand some of the interesting features of human groups and organizations. Social aggregations usually fall into one of five types of gatherings that distinguish themselves as follows:

| SOCIAL AGGREGATION | BOUNDARIES | |
CATEGORY	*External*	*Internal*
Masses	imprecise	imprecise
Crowds	imprecise	imprecise
Parties	yes	no
Groups	yes	yes
Organizations	yes	yes

Masses and crowds are essentially unstructured, although some sociologists' taxonomies show boundarylike entities inside and outside crowds. Parties, groups, and organizations are structured enclaves in which (1) members are distinguished from nonmembers, (2) at least two classes of people are involved, i.e., the leadership and the membership, and (3) some form of discipline and order exists.

POWER INTERPLAY IN THE CORPORATE SETTING

A corporate organization is a differentiated aggregation which is highly structured in the legal corporate form with an owner group, a board of directors, executives, and operating units. Individuals function in separate roles in various units called departments, divisions, or levels with fixed boundaries and memberships. The implicit social contracts in a corporation are the functional or departmental allegiances and relationships which develop between individuals assigned to a particular role. Each person has to identify with the role of their group in order to carry out his or her contribution to the group function. Otherwise, supervision will seek a replacement.

In a network, the allegiance and relationship is optional. The connection may be temporary and a weak tie of common interest. There is no "boss" to remove those who do not cooperate in a network. This is done by individual action to exclude or include others.

Power in a corporate organization is retained or delegated by the board and management to individuals along with responsibility and authority. This hierarchical form is seldom managed properly to utilize the individual's total creative energies and, as a result, some unnecessary stress, conflict, and uncertainty exist. Such command and control by certain persons is absent in a network structure and process. In a network, action is achieved by voluntary cooperation because of mutual trust and shared concern or objectives.

The power interplay in an organized corporate group achieves various degrees of discipline which are not present in a voluntary network. But, it also may accumulate the "stings of command" and function in a business setting on the basis of voluntary captivity (as distinct from a military organization, which is often a less voluntary situation). The psychology involved includes group identification: teamwork, good-of-the-whole aspect, division of labor by policy and subjective preference. Such aspects also express support and reinforce or modify the power interplay.

Beyond that, how the power interplay turns into legitimacy is another important phenomenon. In a structured organization this power is ordered and directed. In a network organization the power is manifest in a state of mind, in attitudes, beliefs, values, and the sharing of influence and perspective.

The enforced condition of the "discipline of promotion" can only be relieved in a corporate organization if a person can demand of others things that were formerly demanded of him or her. One must change places in the system. In promotion, the stings of command which have been accumulated can come out in the open as commands of one's own. In networking, any "commands" are entirely one's own. There are no stings or stingers.

PROFESSIONAL NETWORKING

Professional organizations, in contrast to hierarchical organizations, are also a type of structured enclave. Here, the secret discipline of peer relationships can be as significant as that of hierarchical relationships. At times discipline by one's peers may be even more significant.

Stress, conflict, and uncertainty exist in professional organizations but are of a different nature. Professional firms (1) tend to have an individualized and specialized orientation to key people in the organization (2) have identity and integrity, which is strongly dependent on the identity and integrity of each individual in the firm—their net worth as a professional, (3) tend to be small with diseconomy of size, (4) tend to experience substantial turnover, and (5) have an unusually flexible frame of organizational reference with power relationships being informal and intellectual, and decision making handled by consensus rather than hierarchy. A professional organization functions by networking among professionals, as decided by the peer process.

As an enclave, a professional organization can be viewed structurally in a social continuum. In this regard, the social order may be viewed on a horizontal axis. One end of the continuum represents order, nous, and predictability on the part of the members . . . the domain of hierarchical organizations. Viewed from the other end, the continuum represents disorder, randomness, ignorance, and unpredictability on the part of the members . . . the domain of free-form human networks. The degree of organization is indicated by the extent to which each individual or group is given a specific role, with or without overlapping responsibilities or privileges, and by the position that each individual holds in this graduated spectrum of order-disorder. In a social network, the individual decides for himself or herself where to be positioned, if at all.

NETWORK ORGANIZATION

ADL is a networking-type organization combining four models: (1) the conventional hierarchy required of a corporate entity, (2) a partnership group structure involving professional peer relationships, (3) temporary task forces using a matrix type approach to client assignments, and (4) some collateral, special purpose, organizational entities (e.g., corporate development groups and related sections led by a corporate officer in charge). The organization functions primarily by networking on a person-to-person basis among the professional staff. Social and business contracting and subcontracting goes on constantly in order to assemble necessary talents required for a particular assignment.

ADL may appear, superficially, to be unorganized, but it is organized in multiple ways and works according to its own rules which, in some sense, cause it to be profoundly constrained. The company does have a hierarchy. But creativity being so important to its function, the staff does not let the hierarchy get too efficient. A hierarchy can never be efficient enough (by its own nature) to avoid creating stress, conflict, and uncertainty, all of which dampen creativity.

NETWORKS AND SOCIAL ORDER

One of the most important sources of strength of the Soviet Communist party is its inviolable social contact with the masses. The party, hierarchical in itself, maintains this contact through a network of extensive social organizations.

A contrast to this social contract approach is illustrated in Turkey. There, the "chambers of industry" have been organized differently than in most countries. They are focused on a local geographical basis rather than according to industry. The purpose of this structure is to (1) mediate between the industrialists in the locality and the government for foreign loans and credit and (2) finance industrial investment. These arrangements are actually networks relating government to industry and the financial community.

The sources of social order in Japan stem from the informal controls on individuals. These are exercised by small-scale social groups and networks such as families, fellow workers, and neighbors. Japan's social organizational framework contrasts with American societal structure which fosters a belief in social mobility and results in an impersonal environment.

Japan has a "stable network of named people" which has a great capacity for social control. The network has great influence on social conduct proven by the fact that the per capita incidence of serious crime in the United States is four times the overall rate of crime in Japan. Sociologists attribute this dramatic contrast in the crime rates of two wealthy modern nations to the relative sources of social order. The informal network controls on individuals in Japan are the dominant factor, rather than any differences in modernity, populations, criminal justice system, or violent traditions of the respective nations.

Studies of two different styles of political participation in Nairobi, Kenya, were made during the Independence era, and subsequently in the post-Independence period. The political impact of social networks is interesting. In the period of political independence, the elite mobilized large numbers of individuals to place political pressure on the colonial government. After independence, this mobilization ended and the individuals had to rely on their own resources to remain politically active.

Studies of urban government and nation building in East Africa indicate individual social networks are of three types: (1) kin-based, with limited perceptions about government; (2) association-based, in which the local government is viewed functionally; and (3) ethnic-based, where the government is seen through ethnic values.

Sociologists conclude that local governments fail to penetrate these individual networks and are, therefore, not capable of performing nation-building functions. Viewing social networks' impact on political behavior, sociological analyses of towns in East Africa and elsewhere indicate they may be usefully described as composites of social networks. Empowerment of these networks for political purposes is a particular challenge in the developing world.

The power of hidden social contracts between individuals may be based on national, cultural, ethnic, kinship, religious, economic, or other ties, which in turn may be weak or strong linkages. With the ancient and hereditary forces of human nature dominating our conduct and relationships with one another, a balance of the power of human networking with the command, control, and political forces of structured institutions is the goal to seek in improving large organizational effectiveness.

Chapter 3

How and Why Networks Work

> The more conscious a philosopher is of the
> weak spots of his theory, the more certain
> he is to speak with an air of final authority.
> —*Don Marquis*

I am reminded of the fellow at the bookstore who saw a book entitled *How to Hum*. He bought it and later settled down at home to enjoy it. He was surprised upon opening the package to find that he had purchased Volume 13 of an encyclopedia.

How to network begs the question of what is a network. It is a fact that networks have been working since before we had people who say "I'm from the government and I'm here to help you."

Networks are a form of buddy system that depend on mutual support, not friendship as such. Those persons in any network are there to help themselves by helping each other. There are many scholarly theories about how networks work and why they work. It's all about the way we socialize. The key is mutual support.

Saudi Arabians have one word for it—*diwanniyas*. These are the numerous nighttime social gatherings where people drop in and share coffee and conversation. There is a status element in how many and which *diwanniyas* you cover in one evening. In terms of our culture, *diwanniyas* have somewhat the function of the cocktail circuit.

The Chinese term *guanxi* refers to the complex sociological network of personal relationships that still grease the workings of that society. The network of *guanxi* exercises many forces on interpersonal relationships. One example is that the pressure from family and friends to choose the right spouse is intense. Only 8.4 percent of 462 couples surveyed in Tainjin had married a partner of their own choosing, according to the *Wall Street Journal*. In the 1960's during the Cultural Revolution, humble origins were proclaimed a glory. In that era's egalitarian fervor, *guanxi* moved upper-class people to marry peasants and workers. This movement was a high watermark in people-to-people networking. Hierarchy and rank were bypassed.

THE GRASS ROOTS SIDE OF THE EQUATION

Britain's inner-city problems of physical decay and enormous waste of human talent have generated complex economic and social formulae for regeneration. There is the realization that government on its own—nannyism—will never solve the problems, and that industry and commerce are becoming increasingly ready to help. (Not to be outdone by the British, I am told the situation is so bad in certain United States urban areas that when you call the police they put you on hold and play music. American cities are reckoned to be five to ten years "ahead" of Britain in this urban blight crisis.) Lately in the United Kingdom the grass roots side of the equation has spawned the emergence of the social entrepreneur. Social networking has been rediscovered. Real self-help enterprises are stirring on Merseyside's Weeler Street, at Neath in South Wales, in Sheffield, in the city of London. The ability to teach self-help sensitively at street level takes basic networking skills.

When community life was simpler, self-help was the way things got done. Society's forebearers formed networks because sooner or later they knew that their own survival depended on the willingness of others to help. Neighbors help each other in small town settings in contrast to city apartment dwellers who often don't know or acknowledge persons in the adjacent apartment. Personal exchange is limited to a brief greeting in the elevator, such as, "God isn't dead. He just couldn't find a parking place." Too often there is only an unfocused stare without a word in passing. Detente, the continuation of tension by other means, is a way of city life. This is a sad situation for the millions who long for immortality but do not know what to do with themselves on a rainy Sunday afternoon. We need to reteach how and why networks work. They can be a contributing solution to vexatious, overwhelming social and personal problems.

The effectiveness and management of most organizations unquestionably can be improved by networks and networking. Ambrose Bierce's cynical comment about corporations in the nineteenth century being "ingenious devices for obtaining individual profit without individual responsibility" becomes even more relevant as we approach the twenty-first century. The longer we live the more we realize that the people who want to help themselves can only do so by helping others. It's the basic law of success in human affairs and the underlying notion of networking. People who begin by asking how they can be successful, effective, and happy solely within themselves are doomed from the start. The achievements and rewards go to people who have developed trust in others, are willing to provide something in the way of an asset and, most importantly, recognize the right of others in a network to make demands of them. If you don't have enough to offer or your network contact is wanting or will want too much in return, there is no basis for a network exchange. The network won't work under these conditions.

The purpose of networking is to learn and to give in return. Friendship is often incidental. Again, the social entrepreneur movement in Britain is an interesting example. The movement rests on the simple notion of equity. Since the urban city riots of 1981, the social entrepreneur—a breed of city dweller networkers—has been invented. The *Financial Times* of November 13, 1985, reported that 215 enterprise agencies had developed a handholding role in 16.5 percent of all jobs created. The challenge they face is to train some 200,000 school dropouts a year under the Youth Training Scheme.

The network concept of self-help is crystallized in projects like Instant Muscle, Youth Business Initiative, Neighborhood Energy Action, Project Full-employ, and Youth Enterprise Scheme. These are volunteer-run programs like the Action Resource Centre which draws all sides of society together in a networking partnership to assist disadvantaged young people to help themselves get off the dole queue.

These enterprise projects draw on the business community's know-how and teach self-help sensitively but firmly at street level. The target is the lack of trust and linkage between the disadvantaged, the providers of resources, and these frontline pioneers, the social entrepreneurs who are fashioning these networks of self-interest and interdependence.

The "Wicker" project in Sheffield is probably one of the most successful black self-help enterprises in the United Kingdom. The British Urban Programme has funded an exclusively local workforce to renovate and refurbish an old Georgian building which spans half a block. The local community was adamant that it must control all the funds. More important, it wanted the experience to learn how to mobilize and empower the various segments of the community that existed in a state of tension, conflict, and mistrust. Learning to work together—to network together—over a period of twenty-four months during 1983–1985, the people involved created twenty-four jobs and expect to create thirty-five more upon completion. The new complex provides facilities for cultural education, training, and a small business development center which will be income producing. Best of all is the intangible asset of having created a sensitive living network consisting of those with government resources, industry and business, the disadvantaged, and the community's political leaders. The social entrepreneur—the "networker bee"—has started a model network for social and urban renewal.

One of the most significant accounts of a grass root network was published on the op-ed page of the *Wall Street Journal*, January 17, 1984, and entitled "How Peru Got A Free Market Without Really Trying," by Claudia Rosett. The author is an editor with the Manhattan Institute for Policy Research. A Peruvian think tank, the Institute for Liberty and Democracy (ILD), unearthed facts which overturn the prevailing wisdom that capitalism is a dirty word in Latin America and that an imported economic model helps only the rich and holds no promise for the poor. Fifty-five ILD economists, anthropologists, lawyers, students, and off-duty policemen studied Peru's large underground economy over two-year periods. They accumulated 22,000 documents chronicling the extent of this informal sector and pieced the jigsaw together to see how it works.

The economy was shown not to be the province of the upper class as most people who work in the underground are poor and of Indian extraction. Illegal buses provide 85 percent of Lima's public transportation and illegal taxis provide 10 percent more. Underground activity accounts for 90 percent of the clothing business and 60 percent of the housing construction. Sophisticated structures up to six stories high are built by the underground network of construction firms and workers.

True, bribery is part of the system and access to capital markets is denied. Crude loan pools with high premium rates are the substitute.

The message is that the people of Peru have already chosen a market economy without foreign interference and despite the hindrance of their own government. The Peruvian government has to choose whether to honor the existence of these powerful underground networks or continue to carry out the strange charade, as Ms. Rosett reports, "in which millions of the poor are outlawed for earning an honest productive living."

NETWORK INFORMATION VERSUS COMMUNICATIONS

If we examine the spectrum of pragmatic information based on the concepts of Weizsäcker[1] and Piaget, [2] bureaucratic institutions are on the end of a spectrum where the objective is 100 percent confirmation of information in order to act. Novelty or incompleteness of knowledge are to be avoided. The knowledge level in a bureaucracy is thus comfortable. Information is mainly hard data and comes mostly from internal sources. Knowledge tends to be explicitly related to the order of the day and to defined organizational plans. The official manual of the Internal Revenue Service is an agglomeration of 38,000 pages. It has been described as the world's most confusing publication. Information, yes. Communication, no.

The information in a bureaucracy is often redundant. In a business or government organization the confirmed information consists of reports of results, reports of variance from standard procedures, exeption reports for information. One reason for utilizing networks rather than hierarchical processes in large institutions is that information flows efficiently through organizaitons except that bad news encounters high impedance in flowing upward.

The other end of the information-knowledge spectrum is often a noisy level of external bits of information that travel to those with a lesser need to know. The information often lacks context; it is confusing, random, and mostly "soft" data. The information flows from social encounters, browsing, accidental happenings, grapevines, gossip chains, networking and is in the range of 100 percent not confirmable. It is 100 percent "novelty" information.

The way in which business organizations deal with this end of the information spectrum is by use of macroeconomic forecasts, general threats or opportunity studies, sectoral or subject area identification, and just plain intuitive selection or guessing. Consultants have a field day when the novelty component of information-knowledge is high. Networkers, too, love novel information and communications. They thrive on person-to-person exchanges where there is power in the ability to control or enhance the flow of information and thus affect communications.

Incidentally, the exploding interest in artificial intelligence (AI) applications is in the middle of this information spectrum. Expert systems can provide processes and tools to bridge the gap between 100 percent confirmation and 100 percent novelty ends of the knowledge spectrum. While AI is growing in acceptance, its greatest hurdle, human trust, is the prime asset of the social networking process and something it is most effective in empowering.

There is an important capability in the creating of knowledge as distinct from the mere transfer of information through networking. Creation of knowledge enables a social or political system to constantly recreate its structure to fit the new knowledge level. The social entrepreneurs in Britain are creating knowledge about social renewal. A change of phase in such a social system then occurs through a reformulation or reconceptualization of the variables involved. In the United States the breaking up of AT&T by the Justice Department, while driven by antitrust considerations, introduced a change in phase in the reorganization of the surviving units.

Phase changes in our social system, indicated by the growth in networks and networking in institutions, stress a symbolic perspective of organization. Witness the Sierra Club's image and impact on public opinion as it operates its network. Key features are tribal solidarity, symbolic leaders, and the Sierra Club's dramatic enactments. Coleridge called networks "an interconnected chain or system of immaterial things." The symbolic model of organization is usually visionary and metaphorical and functions largely by informal networking with and around the hierarchy and bureaucracy.

In order for information to be useful it must be accurate and relevant to actual or potential actions. Key information must not be hidden in the mass of total information available or provided. Further, information must be in context with objectives, plans, options, and practices of the organization. Lastly, for information to have substantial business value it must be in the hands of those with authority or license and in a physical position to use and act on the knowledge. This is where most barriers exist. Those with the information are often not in a position to act because of the politics, bureaucracy, and hierarchy.

NETWORK KNOW-HOW

> Austria's highest military decoration—The Order of Maria Theresa—is reserved exclusively for officers who turned the tide of battle by taking matters into their own hands and actively disobeying orders.
> —Watzlawick[3]

Our world's greatest problems are the boundless constraints of our expanding limitations. Network know-how can help our effectiveness in complex organizations by taking the matter of action into our own hands through direct contact. It's not the organization chart; it's the people. It is interesting to note that our physical world, our physical combat actions, and physical systems are energy-bonded. In contrast, our social and political systems are information- and knowledge-bonded. Just as the energy level determines the mode of organization in physical systems, the knowledge and information level defines it for political and social systems, including military organizations. The Order of Maria Theresa is given to people who follow two modes of organization—the chain of command and the local autonomy doctrine. Networking is perhaps the ultimate in local autonomy action. It's a one-on-one theory of action. Networking, eighties' style, is a new look through old lenses at the phenomenon of socializing.

But an even more significant point is that knowledge, unlike energy, is not subject to the first law of thermodynamics. This is the law of conservation of energy. The best you can do is break even, i.e., useful work cannot exceed energy put into it. The second law of thermodynamics asserts that even an ideal engine free of friction losses will see some of its input energy wasted. On the contrary, the knowledge level of the social system is increased by disseminating knowledge. We do not lose knowledge by sharing it with others.

Networks are one of the more interesting ways that information and knowledge are transferred into action. Action can result from networking and it may be swifter and more effective than the action of a hierarchical or bureaucratic process.

Jesse Jackson's unorthodox forays into foreign affairs during the 1984 election campaign bypassed protocol and bureaucracy. While risky and perturbing to the national image, State Department protocol, and our system of sovereign foreign relations, the "networking" action achieved some surprising results in the freeing of prisoners and opening up dialogue on a one-to-one basis.

The lesson is that while it is important to hold on to some of our traditional values and means of accomplishing things, we must learn to let go of some historically valid tenets of how to manage. This is a tightrope-walking exercise. Many of the old ways are inadequate for coping with the change in the organizational phase that is indicated. The knowledge revolution is forcing a new perspective on the criteria for organizational effectiveness.

I'm reminded of the great Wallenda family, the famous high wire circus performers. Even after a single accident killed several members of the Wallenda family, the patriarch, Karl, who was in his seventies, performed on the wire the next day. He carried his sixteen-foot pole for balance as he had carried it since childhood. He had always been told to hold onto his pole—that it would keep him safe and balanced.

Sometime later, Wallenda agreed to walk a high wire ten stories above a city street. It was a windy day, and as he moved onto the wire he started to lose his balance, but he quickly regained control by using his pole and continued across. Then a sudden strong gust of wind came up and he started to fall. He could have caught hold of the wire as he fell past, but he didn't because he was holding tightly onto his pole as he had been taught to do. When he struck a taxi below and was killed, he was still holding that pole.

Those of us in organizations are on a high wire too. Like Karl Wallenda, we are determined to hold onto our "pole," our technology and our concepts of management and organization. We think our only safety lies in them, but we may not survive believing that. We need to let go of some of our learning and "catch the wire" of networks and networking. They won't assure us that our organizations will be safe from the forces of impending change, but at least we will have a chance to struggle back to a position where we can start walking the tightrope of effective organizational action again.

One useful perspective is to recognize and empower networks and facilitate networking within our existing organizations. Network know-how includes not only intuition and common sense about human relations but some fathoming or postulating about how and why networks work.

A THEORY OF NETWORK ACTION

Not a newcomer to the field, the National Science Foundation has supported work in three universities to develop a foundation for constructing a systematic theory of networking. One of the interesting theories, albeit mathematical and scholarly, is that of Ronald S.

Burt, a Columbia University sociology professor. He has two beliefs which form a "fruitful foundation" to his theory of action.[4] One belief is that we all use our resources to realize our personal or group interests, i.e., people are naturally perceptive. We seek to do our "thing." Sort of, the meek shall inherit the earth—if that's okay with you. The second belief is that we all pursue our self-interests in a social context. It is the point of view that living on earth is expensive but it does include a free trip around the sun. The intersection of these two beliefs provides a premise for Professor Burt's structural theory of action—a network model. This theory is primarily about network models or concepts of social structure: perception and action. Simply stated, this means that we as actors are purposive under social structural constraints.

The belief in purposive action is that each person has the right to the product of his or her private property, whether it is in the form of goods or labor. In turn, this right is solely controlled by him or her. Any other actors in the scene, therefore, value this property as a resource rather than a right. This is a powerful notion for there is no fury like a vested interest masquerading as a moral principle.

Given this idealized relationship each of us is motivated to act to improve our well-being. Economists would say that we act to improve our utility. We then evaluate the utility of alternate actions and perform those we perceive as yielding the greatest reward, i.e., enlightened self-interest. Sociologists call this empowering our networks.

Burt's theory of network action means that external social factors determine most courses of network action. We seek a self-interest goal in a friendly environment. Companies with a reputation for career advancement, such as, IBM, ICI, 3M, Citicorp, Merrill Lynch, G.E., Dupont, Sumitomo, ASEA, and Elf Acquitaine, become attractive employers to those applicants who have special talents or "private property" to share.

In addition to fulfilling personal objectives, each individual is motivated by values and beliefs acquired through being part of an organization and adopting its culture, i.e., socialization. Burt's action theory of networking and networks forms a bridge between the personal interests (looking out for number one) and the organization's interests.

Network management requires the ability to combine an appreciation of problem structure and of "opportunity space" with an appreciation of political structure. We have instinct and intuition to size up problems and we move to solve them at the right time depending on the politics of those involved or affected. This skill can be improved with practice and an understanding of the process involved. Our social networks function to ferry support (contact) between particular members of the network. A third dimension of social networking is that of the conflicts involved. Overlaps between conflict, support, and contact exist in models of social networks. Burt's theory copes with this from a mathematical sociologist point of view.

This network action perspective, of bridging individual and organizational interests, derives from whatever mutually rewarding exchanges of property (goods and labor) occur in activities we create in complex organizations in order to get things done efficiently. The concept of membership associations, e.g., National Association of Realtors, the American Chemical Society, Rotary Clubs, and Chambers of Commerce, is to have a structure where the division of labor is widely dispersed among members through committees and advisory groups. Management style is collegial.

These exchanges of personal property (labor) for organizational effectiveness are arbitrary simplifications of behavior considered legitimate under cooperative conduct and action. For example, the subcommittee on surface coatings in the Society of the Plastics Industry (SPI) sets the rules of conduct for SPI members. Burt's network theory postulates the ability of these small groups to act despite the economic, competitive, and societal constraints which impact the plastics industry.

Thus, power and autonomy together underlie transformational change in social structure. This balance of the opposing notions of individual versus collective gain may be powerfully achieved by multiple networking around and along with the hierarchy and bureaucracy. There must be a quid pro quo for those doing the networking and assurance that the institutions are not destroyed. A mutually beneficial exchange of information or property can take place within the social structure of an organization (and in spite of it) by virtue of network actions.

Much of our knowledge of social systems theory comes from the social action system of Talcott Parsons.[5] Networks and networking are but one component of a complete set of artful phenomena dealing with the classic tensions and conflicts of structure versus people.

Along with our intuitive understanding of the importance of social bonds, there is a growing body of knowledge which draws not only on systems theory but also on previous research in such areas as kinships, support systems, adaption to stress, organizational theory, and information exchange. In a small, closely held firm the network properties and relationships of the owners, directors, managers, and employees are intimate, often patriarchical and provincial. Such relationships and personal networks tend to get lost in large organizations.

I am currently consulting with several small- to medium-sized companies in Europe and the United States. The implications of the power and influence of networks are profound. While there are about 14 million businesses in the United States, only 2 million are corporations, about 11 million proprietorships, and 1 million partnerships. Of the corporations, approximately 2 percent are publicly owned, in that shares are traded on stock exchanges. Of the 98 percent of corporations privately owned, many are family firms. The partnerships and proprietorships are held together by social network forces.

The family and partner networks are powerful and present special challenges to stewardship and succession. One company, which must remain unnamed, was founded not by three brothers but by three college students during their school days to provide various services to the student body and faculty. The business boomed and formed a career vehicle for all three for many years. I became involved when the company was approaching $100 million revenue. The margins were shrinking and the captive board of directors was worried about management capability and succession.

The problem condition proved to be focused around the ambiguity of accountability, responsibility, and authority of the three founding top managers. While they were lifelong friends, their trust did not go as far as to accept any one of them as the chief enchilada for the corporation. They each had different complementary talents needed in the business: financial acumen, marketing pizzazz, people sensitivity. Each had internal company networks of followers. The management style was that of plural, rotating leadership. There was a CEO of the month, a chairman, president, and vice chairman. This title wave confused the organization which learned to play games with the shifting decision-making process. For example, capital requests were programmed for submission to be timed with the bias of the CEO of the month.

After analysis of the situation, and a surprisingly friendly reception by the top management, a new chairman was brought in and an outside chief executive officer hired. The gridlock of competing networks of power and influence was dissolved and the founders assumed primary roles as directors only.

Studies show that ethnic, racial, occupational, and socio-economic traps can be perceived as resulting from closed social networks. Looking at it another way, social and occupational mobility can be viewed as the activation or utilization of social links across ethnic, fraternal, familial, or racial boundaries. Power can be seen as flowing through these network linkages. If we trace the networks we see a microsociological perspective of patterns of the exercise of power. Network analysis problems are being progressively solved through the use of such quantitative procedures as path analysis, modeling, and application of many computerized methods. As the *Economist* of April 21, 1984, pointed out, "One of the most welcome things about the computer revolution that began 15 years ago is its habit of undermining centralized authority and controls." Both computer and human networks bypass central authority and controls.

A great deal of attention has been given in corporate governance to the "old boy" network theory which views power in the boardroom as being shared within a system of social relationships between corporate directors—the social class hegemony theory. This differs from the management control theory which considers management to be in total control of an institution. Outside directors are not a majority on the boards of the Fortune 500 corporations. This creates a network of interconnections through interlocking directorates, a factor which is studied extensively and continually by scholars, and the SEC and other regulatory agencies. Much of my consulting practice deals with boardroom networks. They can be constrained by the biases which may occur when there is not a majority of independent directors or trustees overseeing a corporation.

This boardroom network has been visualized as a system through which common norms, values, and a sense of "we-ness" flows. This sense of being part of the corporate establishment can have significant effects on corporate conduct. As a result of the potential power of such networks, boards of directors are a target for activists' movements seeking to make changes in the regulations about boards of directors.

On the other hand, networks within organizations, as well as at the board level, also focus on informal or emergent conditions in organizations which have a positive, motivational effect. In loosely structured organic organizations with a low concentration of authority, emergent coalitions are usually task oriented. Partnerships, federations, family firms, membership associations, learned societies,

professional organizations are examples where networks and networking abound. However, in more mechanistic and militaristic hierarchical organizations, where actions are highly structured, coalitions are also effective. They can become a supportive source for
individuals and an overlay to the hierarchy and bureaucracy. Seldom
are these overlays recognized as such and empowered by the management. The bureaucratic objective is to stamp out networking and
force every action into a controlled system . . . the Orwellian approach rather than a Renaissance orientation.

A National Social Science Research program studied Belgian industry to verify Daniel Bell's hypothesis that in an industrial society
one important consideration of work is primarily the relationship an
employee has with his or her coworkers. The value and significance
of networking was affirmed. Interviews with 975 individuals confirmed that the demands of workers in large Belgian enterprises, for
the most part, exist at a level of unsatisfied aspirations. This was frequently the cause for withdrawal from social interaction and a sense
of unrest.

Studies in Canada, on the other hand, found that social resources
are embedded in a person's social network. Access to better social resources depends on an individual's initial position in the hierarchical
structure and his or her use of weak, rather than strong, ties. The ecological locations—neighborhood, community, outside area—through
which an individual accesses various occupational positions are indeed important.

The essence of network know-how has been and will continue to
be expressed in many scholarly studies of the theories involved. Some
useful explanations to keep in mind about how and why networks
work are: *first*, that people, alone or in groups, are purposive. This
means we use our resources to realize our own interests. *Second*, we
pursue our interests by socializing in the various sectors of organizations and society. *Third*, conflict is inevitable from these two thrusts.
Overlaps occur between objectives, people contacts, support, and
conflict.

The skills of network management enable us to ferry support between network members. This is best done while appreciating the interest of each networker. The politics, the timeliness of the "opportunity space," the impact on the hierarchical structure and process of
the organization: these are the trust and equity components of the
equation to get things accomplished through networks.

Chapter 4

Balancing Networks with Hierarchy

> The Great Chain of Being—formerly a
> lifeline suspended between heaven and
> earth—has been hammered flat, reforged
> into a charm bracelet from which human
> and animal, plant and rock, dangle
> trinketlike in nothingness.
> —*Philip Zaleski[1]*

This flattened cosmos, according to Mr. Zaleski, is obsessed with the lowest common denominator as the highest good "wherein evolution exists only so genes may perpetuate themselves. The gene's carrier, be it worm or human, is nothing more than a disposable wrapper . . . we are all puppets jerked this way and that on strands of DNA." I wouldn't go quite this far but it is true that, as a consequence of scientific advance, meaning has been telescoped down (again) to our individual levels. Values are leveled and, increasingly, hierarchies are being dismantled.

HIERARCHY UNDER SIEGE

This deflation of the globe began a long time ago when we abandoned the "soaring cathedral of medieval cosmology" of Thomas Aquinas for the scientific perspective of a Cartesian-Newtonian world. We have screened out symbolic thought and psychology. This has had an impact on hierarchy as it was known in ancient and medieval times.

Something has been lost in the process of scientific thinking. Institutional purpose often flounders. The hierarchical structures created to channel the efforts of those associated with large organizations are often obsolete and constraining. Some examples are government bureaucracies, military high commands (versus specialized units and guerrilla forces), mammoth universities and corporations (versus smaller colleges and entrepreneurial venture firms), and large hospitals (versus health maintenance organizations or HMOs). The human factor gets lost in giant pyramidal structures even when we try to find it again through decentralization.

Al Giacco, chairman and chief executive officer of Hercules, Inc., describes our current corporate condition: "When you decentralize the hierarchy and wipe out layers of top management, the big problem is who to go to lunch with when the bureaucracy is missing." Individuals need structure and direction. When the hierarchy and ritual are missing, we often become disoriented and seek new totem poles or tribal drills to hang on to. We gravitate towards order, chains of command, ladders of success, class distinction, and pecking order in our search for barnyard reality.

But hierarchy is natural to all social organizations. We have leaders and followers. An effective organization puts its leaders at the top in charge of subordinates who may form subgroups. This is how a hierarchy is created. As this process continues, bureaucracy results. British Petroleum (BP) is perhaps an abnormal example of hierarchical complexity. In 1984, BP had 858 subsidiaries stacked in 12 hierarchical levels.

It is clear that not all hierarchies are equal. Some forms of social structures are more conducive to human development than others. Corporations spend millions of dollars—billions is probably more accurate—to improve human resource effectiveness and corporate culture. Training, development, education, counselling, and employee Christmas party budgets keep growing in attempts to improve organizational effectiveness in large institutions. Despite this, individuals yearn for self-actualization and often spin out to do their own thing. They join smaller firms, go back to school, and generally seek situations where self-realization and the best part of our human nature can find its fullest expression.

The problem can be viewed as one of vertical networks versus horizontal networks. The vertical network is the classical hierarchy, a pyramidal structure which features an up-and-down, linear model of communication. Diffusion of information follows the typical organizational structure passing through successive boxes and levels in the hierarchy.

This top-down communication can be very effective in a military, religious, political, corporate, or other conventionally structured organization. The extension services of the U.S. Department of Agriculture, the Environmental Protective Agency, the Health Services Administration, the U.S. Department of Transportation, the U.S. Postal Service are all mission-type organizations. They employ linear processes of communication for getting things done. This is effective when the top of the organization is clear on the mission and limited adjustments are required in the application of fixed policy, the introduction of hardware or software, or the implementation of technological innovations.

However, when changes in organizational culture, climate, structure, or process take place in complex social systems, top-down, linear communication paths are often inadequate. Behavior, attitudes, beliefs, and comfortable patterns of existence are perturbed.[2] The vertical network can be ineffective in influencing changes and achieving power shifts.

Donald Schön, professor at M.I.T., has done considerable research in horizontal networking and the lateral diffusion of information-exchange.[3] An example of effective horizontal, counter-hierarchical networks is the federally launched Regional Medical Program of the mid-1960's. Grants of $100 million to fifty-five regions in the United States facilitated formation of networks between teaching and research units of university medical schools and community hospitals and practicing physicians.

Other federal government horizontal networking approaches include the National Diffusion Network sponsored during the 1970's by the U.S. Department of Education to promote educational innovation. After three years of operation, 150 innovations had been accepted and adopted by several thousand local schools. Evaluation of these diffusion networks has been a fertile field for academic study.[4]

In the 1970's the National Science Foundation sponsored a horizontal networking approach to assist U.S. cities to utilize innovations from federally approved R&D programs, particularly those in space technology. These networks were user-driven but user-designed. Some crucial urban problems such as traffic gridlocks, crime control, and environmental protection and monitoring have been among those addressed by the programs. Portland, Ann Arbor, and Scottsdale have been cited as particularly effective in urban innovation networking.

The national government in Peking takes an active role in sponsoring horizontal networking processes in China. Diffusion of policy innovations in the People's Republic of China is achieved through local commune, brigade, and county conferences which modify the innovation to fit the local conditions. Mass media assist. Perhaps the most famous local Chinese model is the TACHAI Brigade in Shensi Province. Each year, over 350,000 visitors come to study the Brigade's self-reliant approach to agricultural development.[5]

We can get a sixth-century perspective of this vertical versus horizontal networking debate from Confucius who recognized that the quality of life is dependent on that of human society: to achieve such true humanity, society has to be ordered harmoniously. Confucius believed that the moral ordering of society is expressed in proper hierarchy.

The Confucian concept of hierarchy was based on *lî*, often translated as "rites," "propriety," or "the proper mode of action." In the religious ceremonies of archaic China, the proper order of attendees depended on rank and family relationships. Since the family is the model of hierarchy, we each have multiple roles and relationships: father and mother to son and daughter, husband and wife to each other, son and daughter to parents and in-laws, and so on. Each of us lives in a network of relations which evolve, mature, and expire during our respective life cycles.

Through the centuries, *lî* came to encompass all ritualized elements of human existence including details of etiquette. The *Lî Kî* or *The Record of Ritual* is an encyclopedia of this ceremonial lore.[6] It includes details of traditions, mores, social conventions, amenities, and acts of courtesy. These make civilization possible and enhance our own human dignity and that of others. Only drills, perhaps, in some cases, but symbols, yes, and important ones.

Of all the "Confucius say" one-liners that have been carried down through the ages (or been fabricated by gag writers), I like the real one about sacrificing a sheep. At the beginning of the month the sacrifice was made to bring ancestors to mind, making them psychologically if not actually present. The continued reminder of one's debt to one's ancestors was sufficient reason for the ceremony in honor of the ancestral spirits. When one of his disciples suggested it was unnecessary to sacrifice a sheep each month, Confucius replied, "You love the sheep, I love the ceremony."[7]

UNDERSTANDING HIERARCHIES

A hierarchy is any established order based on value, status, rank, importance, relativity, personal taste or natural law. Hierarchies may be subjective (my club is better than your club), or universally recognized and constant (the pilot captain is in charge of the aircraft).

There is a human ecology in Times Square which is at least as elaborate and as fascinating as the ecology of the tropical jungle—to which the area has often been compared. Different territories in Times Square mark not only different occupations but different levels of status as well. Street people stake out fixed spots or hangouts where members of their own kind preside. For example, elderly male residents of single-room occupancy hotels gather near subway stops or shoeshine stands.

Another type of turf is the hustling spot, set up like a nomad's camp where those running con games, selling phony jewelry, or shoplifting, exist by pursuing a host of activities requiring good street sense and an aptitude for calculating the risks of arrest, injury, or being taken in by someone else's "game."

In these various territories there are hierarchical levels of occupational status. Street people have a hierarchy in which the mentally ill and alcoholics occupy the bottom rung. Young male hustlers are further up, and pimps who set up shop in bars—safe from arrest and other dangers outside—are an admired elite at the top.[8]

Each of these status groups share norms and rituals learned in prison and the ghettos. The Times Square "cleanup" plan, the result of massive building redevelopment projects which hope to salvage this valuable Manhattan real estate, will alter the terrain substantially. Street people will relocate to other areas but their hierarchies will survive as a socially established ordering of human relationships.

Boundaries are established by hierarchies as are incentives to make the grade, move up the organization, sit in the front row, be recognized by the elite as you go through the reception line, or be in front of the academic procession. The symbols of academic costumes punctuate the overlapping pyramids of distinction based on a code of academic dress formulated at Columbia University in 1895. Although most all gowned academics wear mortarboards, the tassels vary in color and the hoods have distinctive coloration that tells most about the wearer. Doctor's hoods are four feet in length, master's and bachelor's hoods are three-and-a-half feet and three feet long, respectively.

We grow up thinking in hierarchies, understandably, as our family units are hierarchical. Our language and colloquialisms epitomize hierarchy with such expressions as *upper crust*, *hobnob*, and *cream of the crop*. The word *hierarchy* has Greek roots . . . *hieros*, meaning sacred, and *archos*, meaning leader. High priest in Greek is *hieraeches*. As Lisbeth Mark notes in her book: "In the hierarchy of the Roman Catholic Church, the angels rank just below God Himself (or Herself) . . ." and they in turn are grouped according to their own nine levels starting with seraphim, ratcheting down to the lesser archangels and just plain angels.[9]

While each of us may have our own guardian angel, life has become so complicated that we can no longer evade the responsibility of our own survival. Thus, we need to understand hierarchies, their importance, value, and limitations. In our increasingly complex, constraining society there are mounting instability and irrational trends which put conventional hierarchy under siege. This is when human networks spawn.

As systems grow in size and complexity they reach a limit where a new level of hierarchical control is required to allow the system to function reliably. Contacts jump from about one hundred possibilities for an executive with five people reporting to him or her to over one thousand when he or she has eight subordinates. Networks of different relations overlap in these evolving organizational systems, and multiple hierarchies are created which form networks of different hierarchic relationships. The dynamics get overcomplex and cause an evolution of new hierarchical simplifications. Those of us in hierarchical corporations can become demotivated or overwhelmed by the layers of organization and controls above us. We often seek satisfaction, recognition, and understanding around smaller company cliques or "tribal groups." These include organized labor unions, social clubs, and professional societies, both within and outside of our corporations.[10]

It is helpful in understanding hierarchies and networks to pursue the systems view. The systems experts generalize about hierarchies in a manner divorced from the vertical authority structure originally denoted in human organizations starting with the family unit. Hierarchical architecture (in systems language) simply means a set of Chinese boxes of a particular kind. One box encloses a second box, which in turn encloses a third, and so on. The recursion continues as long as the patience of the craftsman holds out. Thus, when we open one Chinese box we behold a whole small set of boxes. Each time we open up a box we see a new set. The series is a sequence and a hierarchy is a partial ordering—specifically, a tree of relationships or interconnections . . . a special kind of network.

David K. Hurst, executive vice president of Russelsteel, Inc., a subsidiary of Federal Industries Ltd., Canada, found his company in a 100 percent leveraged buyout and then merged with a large unprofitable steel fabricator. The steel company had essentially no managerial rules, few resources, and little management strength. The Russelsteel managers, accustomed to working with hard facts, rigid organizational structure, and hard numbers, found their "hard box" way of managing a total misfit with the merged company culture and style. In order to deal with these circumstances, the new managers had to adopt another managerial mode: the soft bubble of process.[11]

The soft, intuitive framework offered a counterpart to the hard, hierarchical framework, and roles became counterparts of tasks, groups replaced structure, networks operated instead of information systems, and "rewards were soft instead of hard." People were "viewed as social animals rather than as rational beings." Jung's "yearnings to be led" manifested themselves.

The management process was made to work as motivating rewards were applied to persons playing necessary roles and working together as groups. These groups were characterized by open communication and linked by networks through the organization. Mr. Hurst observed: "The immediate product is a high degree of mutual trust. This trust allows groups to develop a shared vision that in turn enhances a sense of common purpose." Individuals felt they had a mission of their own which "was spiritual in the sense of being an important effort much larger than oneself."

Mr. Hurst, after three years of learning to do things differently, reaches to the Taoists for explanations. The polarities of hierarchical hard box structure and the "soft bubbles" of trust and networking were balanced components of this experience.

HUMAN NETWORKS: A NEW DIMENSION IN CORPORATE HUMAN-RESOURCE MANAGEMENT

The relatively recent discovery of the technical nature, dynamics, and significance of social (hi-touch) networks within and outside of our institutions presents a preview of how some corporate organizations will learn to work more effectively in the future. Research and development departments, human resources, marketing, and corporate relations are obvious beneficiaries of networking applications.

Innovative leaders are exploring the networking dimension of human resource management in their corporations. It is important to track the trends of emerging research and development on social networking and the phenomenon's impact on corporate organizations. Progressive corporations are constantly seeking better relationships with their environment and their stakeholders. To do this companies need to improve the physics of their organization plus the climate and texture of company culture, all of which contribute to creativity and innovation. Networks and networking are useful concepts and can be significant resources to cope with both condition-driven and ambition-driven corporate strategies.

Informal social networks always have existed in large organizations, and usually have had a vital role in the spread of organizational information culture. Recently, there have been some changes in the texture of these networks that are attracting considerable attention.

Everett M. Rogers, professor at the Institute for Communication Research of Stanford University, and D. Lawrence Kincaid, professor at the East-West Communication Institute in Honolulu, Hawaii, have been leaders in the search for a new paradigm for communication theory and network research. Their 1973 study of human communication networks in a highly successful development program in the Republic of Korea formed the basis for their recent book.[12] A strategy for mobilizing interpersonal networks through 28,000 Korean mothers' clubs totalling 750,000 members was devised as a village woman-power process of mutual information exchange. The major problems of rural Korea were exemplified by overpopulation, poverty, lack of cooperative trust, and underdevelopment. The emphasis on communication links, rather than on isolated individuals, in the village of Oryu Li, near Seoul, enabled the exploration of the influence of other individuals on human behavior, without being too mathematical as most prior network analyses tend to be. A remarkable record of family planning adoption, community development, and financial progress was achieved through the creation of effective communication networks established as a result of the field research study.

The literature on social networks is vast and tends to be dominated by methodologies, formulae, and techniques. Rogers notes the sign in one fellow scholar's office: "Network analysis is the answer, but what was the question?"[13]

Rogers and Kincaid's analyses set forth four main concepts on which they based their approach to communication structure: connectedness, integration, diversity, and openness. Network analysis is a means of investigating behavior in a human system at a macro level of communication links. It focuses on the communication-social structure and process within which people live. The authors make these elements visible and subject to variations. Their major theme is that communications networks can be conceptualized theoretically, studied empirically and managed personally. The theme jibes well with the thrust of this book: if we balance hierarchy with networks we can manage more effectively.

Social movements have spawned some interesting networks and coalitions of kindred souls to create subcultures or platforms to cope with social change. Such movements usually advocate decentralized power, personal growth, global cooperation, ecological harmony, and other "good things." Their goals are seductively attractive: resurgence of local leadership, self-reliance, and self-fulfillment. Networks seek to take back some of the powers that have been delegated to impersonal governments and large corporations.

It is important that managers and directors recognize and understand the movements underway so that their companies benefit from certain shifts in hierarchy and bureaucracy. Both classical hierarchies and network models have vital roles. They can exist coetaneously if the inherent conflicts in communications, and command and control processes are understood and resolved. The challenge is not to stamp out the "new hi-touch politic," but to engage it effectively within and without our institutionalized organizations.

An innovative use of a business organization's positional and attribute networks was announced in November 1984 by Dow Chemical Company. The positional network consisted of all 26,000 persons in the United States who were employed by Dow. Their positions were linked by hierarchy and function within the Dow organization. The attribute network consisted of those 134,000 persons who were characterized as shareowners of Dow stock. As owners they had a common property or attribute.

The notion of using employee and shareowner constituencies to support a common interest was first mentioned about ten years ago by educator Irving Kristol at a semiannual meeting of the Chemical Manufacturers Association (then Manufacturing Chemists Association). He advised chemical companies to develop a constituency to help out with their public image and other problems. Given the industrial disaster in Bhopal, India, and in Mexico during 1984, this advice has even more merit today than when it was first offered.

A $1 million grant from Dow Chemical was awarded to the Washington, D.C.-based private foundation American Council on Transplantation (ACT) in order to "do something that would respond to a significant and tangible national need," explained Robert W. Lundeen, Dow's board chairman. "But," Lundeen continued, "a condition that we made for ourselves [is that] it can't be something where Dow can gain commercially." Dow, doing no research in the field nor manufacturing any products or pharmaceuticals that are involved in transplantation, has no commercial connection at all in the ACT program.

Less than half of the 100,000 Americans who might have benefited from organ or tissue transplants last year received them. ACT requires financial assistance to get an informational program off the ground. Dow plans an in-house donor education program on transplantation, with audiovisual presentations for use by both Dow employees and community groups. Personal messages, via quarterly reports, will carry the message to Dow shareowners.

This program exemplifies volunteer and private sector action at its best. I hope that other business organizations will follow this lead in using their powerful positional and attribute networks to illustrate their commitment to critical social needs.

SOCIAL MOVEMENTS: SOME DRIVING FORCES

Changes in our basic value systems are constantly occurring. On a global scale there is a strong drive toward egalitarianism resulting from the growth and affluence of developed nations. However, this affluence was achieved by a growth in interdependence among nations which, in turn, has created a search by individuals and institutions for a stronger sense of identity. Human potential (personal and spiritual) networks are peculiarly American and children of the post-industrial information age. Examples of such networks are: American Humanist Association, Cooperative Communities of America, Women Outdoors, Esalen Institute, North American Network of Women Runners, World University, and Society for Human and Spiritual Understanding.

The process by which technology is made socially relevant is an elusive one. Every new technological impact has a compensatory social and human response. Defining this impact is troublesome because, *first*, those in specialized fields usually can't agree on the basic context in which the impact should be assessed; *second*, finding a common purpose is difficult if not impossible; *third*, the pace of development requires a degree of technological knowledge rarely linked to economic, social, and political understanding; and *fourth*, social and human response movements take longer than many of our technological advances. This is true even though there is a substantial lag—eight to fifteen years—between the time technical information is generated and the time it is normally used in a technological innovation. It is important to remember that from 60 to 80 percent of significant technological innovations have been in response to market demands and social needs. The remaining 20 to 40 percent have originated in response to new scientific or technological advances and opportunities.

Recently, an embryonic hi-touch human response movement has emerged, partially operated by social reform networks. One reason such networks have arisen is that social complexity, social pressures, and political imperatives are challenging those institutions and persons who want to manage our affairs with a technological-economic star as sole reference. Examples of these networks include: National Indian Youth Council, National Association for the Advancement of Colored People (NAACP); Association of Community Organizations for Reform Now (ACORN); A Citizen's Organization for a Sane World (SANE); Institute of World Order; Movements for a New Society (MNS); Institute for Social Justice; Amnesty International; and Common Cause.

When the world was a simpler place in which to live, the externalities and interconnectedness were more immediate but just as critical to human experience. The social hi-touch movements underway now, which rely on relatively open-ended networks of communication and the sharing of concerns and goals, are causing social transformation in corporations, other institutions, and society at large. Hierarchies have failed to solve many of society's problems so networks are taking root in various movements to cope with the social issues both within and outside existing institutions. As a result, a general decoupling process is taking place as individuals retreat from (or work around) the complexities of life in corporations, government, and other institutions.

Further, there is a recognition of "social traps," the tendency of organizations to start in a direction that ultimately proves unacceptable but which cannot be reversed without causing even greater problems (e.g., exploitation of limited resources, disposal of wastes, undue reliance on technology). Social reform organizations are then formed to encourage action to deal with these problems. Examples of social reform organizations include: Clamshell and Abalone Alliances, Sierra Club, Greenpeace, Union of Concerned Scientists (USC), Western Solar Utilization Network (Western Sun), and Alternative Energy Resources Organization, Montana (AERO).

The peculiarly British invention of the "old boy network" (OBN) is "a club without premises, constitution, or life membership—Not simply a clique. Not quite an élite. Not exactly a trade union. But with some of the qualities of all these alliances," according to the London *Sunday Times* journalist Nicholas Tomalin.[14] The OBN operates through contacts with a friend (originally from school), instead of through the usual channels—it is a bureaucracy-buster, a queue-jumper, and a red-tape cutter. Such networks offer the tribal security of an interconnected mesh of contacts not only in school, the military, business, government, and the professions, but in society in general.

The social networks we are particularly concerned with are change-directed structures affecting future corporate effectiveness. They differ from the OBNs. Elite university circles, royal alliances, private clubs, boards of directors, and corporate establishment groups are OBNs which still dominate large numbers of people. In contrast, the emerging social hi-touch networks bypass the OBNs by weaving webs of awareness at various levels of activity. They seek to create new means to address issues challenging corporate effectiveness, such as, loss of individual identity, lack of motivation, and bureaucratic decision processes.

While sociologists and anthropologists have used the network concept as a metaphor for one hundred years, it was not until 1965 when anthropologists were studying church and black power movements that they found that other movements (e.g., civil rights, environmental, antiwar) showed common patterns of behavior. These patterns can be used constructively in corporations, other institutions, and affinity groups, such as professional organizations, to improve creativity, motivation, fulfillment, and performance effectiveness if the nature and dynamics of the change-directed networks are understood.

Since the 1965 findings of the anthropologists there has been more awareness of the value of networking in complex organizations. As a consequence, universities, learned societies, and consultants are researching social networks and networking processes to develop algorithms, software, new applications, and relevant data sets. For example, a recent social network conference produced papers on emergent network properties, statistical network models, organizational networks, social networks in ethical relations, network analysis in historical research, social support networks, communications and computer networks, network measurement, and other network-related topics.

Networks are seldom independent centers of power. Thus, they are dependent on social context. This means special management attention must be paid to corporate climate and texture, philosophy, structure, process, ethics, and values. Cliquishness, elitism, power groups, "the establishment," and conservative political characteristics are common in many informal networks. These attributes (i.e., characteristics) may be counterproductive when attempting to effect change in complex organizations or systems. Networks need to avoid these typical attributes if they are to cope with hierarchy and bureaucracy.

Barter is the usual mode of exchange in a network. Information is given and received. Networks can function rapidly or have a long time delay. Managers who tolerate or enhance networking in a hierarchical organization should take into consideration the potential cost elements, although in general, informal networks often afford a low-cost way of getting things done or effecting change in a complex system if information and opportunities are plentiful.

While human nature causes us to seek hierarchies to provide order and assign everything and everyone to their place, we rebel against straitjacket classifications. There is constant tension between the notions that we may be created equal and the drive to be the chief enchilada rather than low man on the totem pole.

> The heavens themselves, the planets, and this centre
> Observe degree, priority, and place,
> Insisture, course, proportion, season, form,
> Office, and custom, in all line of order.
> —William Shakespeare, *Troilus and Cressida*,
> Act I, Scene III

Chapter 5

The Bureaucratic Bypass

> After a decade we have reached a plateau
> of activity that cannot be a comfortable
> resting place for the next decade. We have
> to aspire higher; higher quality, more
> relevance, more worldly impact. I believe
> that this can best be achieved if the
> National Member Organizations organize
> their own internal infrastructures to
> encourage more collaborative networking.
> —*Howard Raiffa*
> *Founding Director, IIASA*

Professor Raiffa, Frank P. Ramsey Professor of Managerial Economics at the Graduate School of Business Administration and the John F. Kennedy School of Government at Harvard University, was the founding director of the International Institute for Applied Systems Analysis (IIASA), Laxenburg, Austria. His statement in Options, Summer 1984, was directed at the world's "Big Problems and a Small Institute," even though there are 452 institutional members in the twelve-nation IIASA network organization.

The world's problems, which are the research targets of IIASA, are not new, only bigger and more intertwined. Sir E. B. Tylor observed, "There is no human idea as long ago in time or as far away in distance as to have broken its connection with us now and here."[1]

BUREAUCRACY VERSUS NETWORKS

Whether our institutions are dealing with old ideas or new problems, there is an inexorable tendency toward hierarchical structure and the building of bureaucracies. The only thing that saves us from these bureaucracies in the long pull is their inefficiency. A more immediate relief is networking which is the antidote to hierarchical impedance and a process for bypassing bureaucracy.

Canadian-born psychoanalyst Elliott Jacques, Ph.D., head of the School of Social Institutions at Brunel University in London, has studied stress and pressure in various corporate management systems. Jacques estimates that "in the United States more than 75 percent of the working population is packed into bureaucratic hierarchies. On balance, these hierarchies—as managed at the present time—*do* change people negatively."

A 1984 report from the International Monetary Fund makes an interesting international comparison of the numbers, salaries and conditions of the civil service bureaucracies. Britain has more bureaucrats in relation to its size, population, and living standards than any developed country except Sweden. Since the 1979 Thatcher election, the British Civil Service staff is down 14 percent to less than 630,000. The peak was 746,161 in 1972.[2] Government employees per capita indices (number of public sector employees per hundred inhabitants of developed countries in 1983) show double digit ratios for Sweden at 16.31; United Kingdom 13.21; Denmark 12.58; Australia 10.97; New Zealand 10.35. Single digit indices: Belgium 8.77; United States 8.07; Canada 7.80; West Germany 7.70; and Japan at 4.44.

Total government employment per capita tends to increase as per capita income rises. The relationship is particularly strong for countries with a per capita income in excess of U.S. $800. On the other hand, the share of central government employment in total non-agricultural employment declines with per capita income; for countries with a per capita income of less than U.S. $1400, the share of total general government employment declines; above that income level, it increases.[3]

The difference between networks and traditional bureaucracies is the extent to which the individuals in the system interconnect. Noel McInnis, former managing editor of *Brain/Mind Bulletin*, points out some interesting things if we change to a weblike structure from the geometric pattern of a typical pyramidal, hierarchical organization with its levels of bureaucracy and cascade of organizational boxes.[4] The reformed weblike structure places the former top of the pyramid as the center of the web. The subordinate chains of command then radiate out, spokelike, in all directions along with their subsidiary branching. With such a web pattern we can see the vulnerability of this traditional bureaucratic structure. If the central focus is destroyed, the bureaucratic web model will not hold together as the various radii and branches will not be interconnected anymore. If a branch node is destroyed the branch and its derivative branches are lost to the pattern as they have no horizontal or other directional connections with the overall organizational web design. It's like having no rim on the spokes of a wheel. When a spoke is severed there is no other connection to retain it in the structure.

In contrast, if the organizational relationships are designed in the form of a spiderweb structure, the spiderweb can survive total destruction of any one of its nodes, including the center, due to the extensive interconnectivity which maximizes flexibility and minimizes vulnerability of the pattern. The power of a spiderweb network is distributed polycentrically rather than concentrated monocentrically as in a classical hierarchical structure. The strength of a network will tend to be proportionate to the interconnectivity among its members. The strength of a hierarchical structure is in position power up and down the chain of command. The power flows and is either delegated or withheld, depending on status differentials.

In early 1984, two business women in their twenties took the initiative to form a new career network for young women in New York City. Tracy M. McDonald and Karen A. Page, friends, roommates, and interns at Kuhn Loeb, felt a need to meet peers in other companies who had similar high career aspirations but who had difficulty in their own hierarchical organizations getting other ambitious women to exchange ideas and break their sense of isolation. The Young Women's Forum of New York (505 Court Street, Suite 5F, Brooklyn, New York 11231) was initially thought of as a group of about twenty people. But while compiling a mailing list, McDonald and Page deemed that there were 500 potential members. Criteria were established for admission: a bachelor's degree in arts or science, a professional position in any field, a recommendation by at least one woman who was already a member of the network, and "high career aspirations."

According to the *New York Times*, July 30, 1984, the Forum meets regularly for dinner discussion meetings, to hear speakers, and, in general, to share concerns and plans. Thus, a new human network was born to bypass unresponsive hierarchies.

THE ADAPTIVE MAGIC OF NETWORKS

Bureaucracy is a social invention. It relies exclusively on the power to influence through reason, rules, and law and was developed as a reaction against the managerial practices in the early days of the industrial revolution. Man's true hope, it was thought, lay in his ability to use his head as well as his hands and his heart. Thus, social roles were institutionalized and reinforced by legal tradition rather than by cult of personality. Emphasis was placed on competence rather than arbitrary whims.

Bureaucracy oversimplifies organizational dynamics and rests its case on impersonality of interpersonal relations in such matters as: division of labor (based on functional specialization); a defined hierarchy of authority; systems of rules and procedures concerning individual rights, duties, and work situations; and promotion and selection on technical competence. Bureaucracy thrives on a highly competitive, undifferentiated, and stable environment. It is particularly suitable for routinized tasks.

One Sunday at our cottage on Lake Sunapee in New Hampshire, I got to thinking about the power of bureaucracy and hierarchy. I looked over "the waters of the wild goose," or Soo Nipi as the Penacook Indians called Lake Sunapee. Some geese were flying south in their traditional "vee" formation. What beautiful geometry of the hierarchical flying pyramid—a demonstration of a group effectively in action.

Ornithologists tell us that geese get 71 percent more flying range and greater altitude in this "vee" formation. This is due to the updraft created behind each goose's wing action. Another interesting observation given by scientists concerns the honking of the geese in formation. Usually those in the rear of the formation do the honking indicating support for the leaders as they drive this winged salient toward a common destination. The leaders need occasional "honking-on" from those lower in the hierarchy.

The group effectiveness and support is further evidenced when one of the geese falls out of formation for whatever reason, including gunshot pellets. The fallen one is accompanied to the ground by two other geese who stay with him until he can resume attempts to catch up or expires. The updraft of mutual support of a hierarchy directed to a common objective can be powerful.

But a problem exists when the environment is destabilized and uncertain. Bureaucracy and hierarchy are often incapable of managing the stress, discontinuities, and tension between personal goals and corporate goals and of adapting to new sets of conditions.

Enter the invention of social or human networks. Not a new social structure but one with temporary, adaptive characteristics with emphasis on the individual. Any organization will be organic in nature and style. The networks evolve when groups of relative strangers with a set of diverse skills respond to a problem or condition. This is distinct from programmed goals and role expectations which typify a bureaucracy or hierarchy. Warren Bennis, social psychologist and prolific author, uses the description "organic-adaptive structure" to characterize these temporary systems of diverse specialists who make up task forces and networks to get around hierarchical and bureaucratic inadequacies. Bennis disagrees with the viewpoint that these organizational forms represent a "new Bohemianism" in which leisure—not work—becomes the emotional-creative sphere of life:

> Bureaucracy with its "surplus repression" was a monumental discovery for harnessing muscle power *via* guilt and instinctual renunciation. In today's world, it is a lifeless crutch that is no longer useful. For we now require structures of freedom to permit the expression of play and imagination and to exploit the new pleasure of work.[5]

Any social sorcery using networks to bypass or provoke a further evolution of bureaucracies will break down the walls between knowledge and power. Bureaucracies and hierarchies do not promote a free flow of information, ideas, or reactions. In an information age, the systems which process information most effectively are the ones most likely to survive. When knowing what's going on and what to do means having power, networks are more likely to be favored as a "magic" way of getting something done.

It is not happenstance that in a 1984 study we found a common positive attribute of ten innovative companies: an organizational style with easy communication and human networking. The art of innovation depends on a changing series of champions. The champions network directly with different elements of the organization and environment in which they exist. The bureaucratic and hierarchical power flow are short-circuited by collaboration with those who really know . . . the GWRK's mentioned in Chapter 1.

Since thinking seriously about networks and networking, I have been alert to examples of unusual and interesting networks that have come to my attention. The number of existing networks is legion and their variety is unbelievable. As an example, *Networking: The First Report And Directory* lists 1,526 networks in seven categories: Healing (health and the life cycle), Sharing (communities and cooperatives), Using (ecology and energy), Valuing (politics and economies), and Evolving (global and futures). Tim Heald's book, *Networks*, lists Great British Networks, Old School Ties, and the Massingberd Dynasties of England and Wales as typical of the "old boy network" scene in the United Kingdom.[6]

The following are eight randomly selected species of networks which I find significant in the field of rapidly growing human networks. They continue to spring up like wildflowers in and across many lands in spite of the continued creation of more formal institutions.

The origin-of-the-species network was, of course, the family. This is a good place to start. Families were around long before there were bureaucracies to bypass, and the prime responsibility for family planning in our society rests with the family unit. The family influences the early socialization and future of its children.

FAMILY NETWORKS

Father, mother, and children are for each other the principal source of affective (emotional) and ascriptive (attributed) relationships. They can call upon the grandparents, aunts, uncles, cousins, and in-laws for help and information. As each sibling marries, the family expands, and there is, theoretically, the possibility for infinite expansion limited only by intermarriage. These traditional "nuclear families" wield considerable power and influence, and their expectations are boundless. The family party line can call on Aunt Betty in Brookline, who is certain that Cousin George's real estate firm in San Francisco will be able to find a house for Clara's Sally, who's moving to Fresno.

Each individual family member has a network of his or her own from school days through business and community associations, but kinship is usually the first source to turn to. The kinship system becomes a recruitment base, organized around blood and family ties. Families lack formal structure and definable boundaries, but tradition seems to demand instant recognition of members of the family and knowledge of where each lives, if married, how the business is, and when they will be in the market for more insurance, etc. There is commonly one member of the family that keeps track of the others, even the black sheep.

Some family networks are highly connected and others are dispersed as shown in figure 5.1. A high degree of connectedness obviously occurs in concentrations of persons of the same or similar occupations in a local area with low population turnover and continuity of relationships. Even in highly connected family units, some members may not communicate or be on social terms with each other. With our social world becoming mobile and families dispersed by vocational relocation, the traditional nuclear family may suffer. The dispersed family, however, may find it easier to stay connected because of the better communication and travel facilities.

The external social friendships of family members form networks that are distinct from organized groups that have common aims, interdependent roles, and distinctive subcultures. Only some, but not all, of the component individuals of a network have social relationships with each other. The component external units have no external boundary and do not necessarily make up a larger social whole.

The total network of the family plus its external units is impressive and often tempts the family to make multiple and pressing demands on its members. The response differs among families and changing times. Responding to demands can influence a member's ability to participate in and meet the role demands of other collectives, such as associations, institutions, clubs, and nations. Unresponsive family members, changes in marriage customs, and shrinking of family size have led to predictable results in recent years.

NEW SURROGATE FAMILY NETWORKS

The Carnegie Council on Children found that a staggering change has occurred in families during the last quarter century. Their research notes that today all families need help of some kind once in a while. With the decline of nuclear families many are left without traditional sources of support. Community volunteers must come to the aid of families in crisis and serve as family support networks. These support networks should not only solve problems but help to enrich lives.[7]

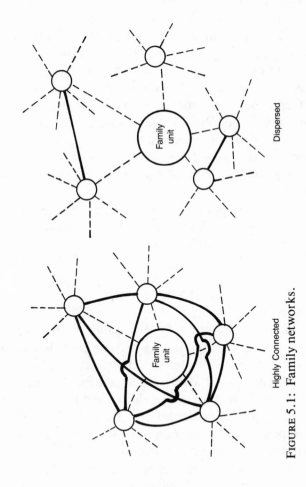

Family
unit

Highly Connected

Family
unit

Dispersed

FIGURE 5.1: Family networks.

In my former hometown of Springfield, Massachusetts, the Downey Side program has, for a decade, persuaded ordinary families to adopt older teenage delinquents to keep them out of prison or trouble. With the help of support networks the adopting family can succeed at this enormously difficult task and accomplish transformations in the lives of delinquents. The Downey Side families get together regularly to share and evaluate successes and failures. They encourage each other and the teenagers involved.

The hospice movement throughout the United States represents another remarkable family support network. It focuses on the terminally ill. Families facing terminal illness of one of their members often lack the emotional and physical energy to cope or even to know where to start to get help. Energy replenishment is the essential contribution of a support network of physicians, psychologists, clergy, social workers, and volunteers.

Gamblers Anonymous is a network that operates much in the same way as Alcoholics Anonymous. Members of GA "talk each other down" in an emergency and reduce the tension or stress that leads to a gambler's impulsive behavior. The gambler finds security in being with a group of people who understand compulsive gambling.[8]

Volunteer support networks often come about through churches, councils on aging, child care centers, and small groups that see a need and work together to help individuals.

HISTORICAL FAMILY NETWORKS

During the period of the British mandate, the Palestinians, who perceived foreign occupation as divisive and destructive, retreated to family networks in order to preserve the elements which enhanced unity, heritage, and identity. The Sharish, a religious law and dominant force in the Moslem world, lacked linkage to public policy and was tailored to individual needs. Islam provided the family unit, the paramount social structure, with the necessary strength to make an effective, unifying mechanism.

An unusually homogeneous traditional folk culture existed in Central Ostrobothia Province in Western Poland during the 1800's and developed from Finnish influences. The social base was an egalitarian society of small farmers who lived in extended family networks. They often worked under formal cooperative agreements and were distinct from upper-class craft societies, and music and dance performing groups.

While it is said that the Code Napoleon caused the extinction of tacit communications held together by family networks in the region of Thiers in Auvergne, France, more recent studies have shown that the appearance, permanence, and decline of such family network communities can be explained by social and economic conditions in the region. The real network existed within the manorial system in the region.

SCIENTIFIC INSTITUTIONAL NETWORKS

IIASA, mentioned at the beginning of this chapter, is an interesting example of a scientific network. It is a nongovernmental, multidisciplinary research institution, founded in 1972, which brings together scientists from around the world to work on problems of common concern. By 1984, 452 institutions from around the world had become National Member Organizations. The further development of a network of collaborating institutions is a matter of prime importance to the Institute which historically has conducted research in seven topics: economy, environment, energy, food, population, science and technology, and system and decision sciences.

Network New York sets up an informal pattern of communication for the scientific community within the geographical area of greater New York City. New York has the largest scientific community in the United States. There is hardly a scientific institution in the city that does not have one or more of its members on the adjunct faculty of the Rockefeller University. Adjunct faculty members work in close collaboration—intellectually and, as often as not, at the bench—with the regular Rockefeller faculty.[9]

Notes of seminars, colloquia, and other lectures are freely disseminated among the major institutions in the city. Outside visitors often attend. The grapevine signals presence of prominent scientists visiting from outside of New York. It is important to note that these communications are not formally organized.

In contrast to New York, the specialized science centers in cities elsewhere are dominated by one or two majestic institutions. Communication among scholars becomes part of the academic tradition and structure of each institution. Outside the United States, particularly in the USSR, scientific effort tends to be organized more formally under government direction. The federal laboratories around Washington, D.C. follow this model.

There are several organizations within the New York area which are formally organized, i.e., the New York Academy of Sciences and the New York Academy of Medicine. The increasing congestion in the city, the hazards of city life, and external pressures for specialization in parts of the informal network presage a further regionalization effort with patterns of communications tending to embrace clusters of related institutions within easy walking distance. The networks will continue in archipelago form as the respective "islands" of scientific interest continue networking.

An interesting comparison of the locations of authors of scientific publications reflects that other cities have more productive author networks. The number of primary authors in a city per 1,000 people, according to a 1974 study, is as follows: Cambridge, Massachusetts 14.50; Berkeley, California 11.00; Washington 1.21; Prague 1.19; Moscow 1.07; Munich 0.94; Kiev 0.79; Boston 0.71; London 0.59; Leningrad 0.57. Networking by written communication exhibits a different root pattern than the verbal networking typical of the scientific "Network New York" model.

Without fanfare in September 1982, the first-ever two-way satellite link between the United States and the Soviet Union permitted live transmission of music between the two countries. May 1983 saw the feat repeated with a first-ever, live two-way exchange between Soviet and American citizens, astronauts, cosmonauts, educators, and politicians. Late in 1983, a third link-up occurred between children in both cultures when the Moscow Film Festival was directly connected to a group at the University of California in San Diego. And, also in the same year, physicists and biologists in Washington and Moscow were linked by satellite to discuss biological consequences of nuclear war. In the Spring of 1984, the Institute of Noetic Sciences, in Sausalito, California, began sponsoring a $100,000 television documentary "Linking Us Together," the story of how Track II—or people-to-people diplomacy—has accomplished this unprecedented development in international relations.

SHADOW NETWORKS

In his book *Beyond the Stable State*, M.I.T. professor Donald A. Schön introduces the concept of a shadow network. A shadow network is a network that fills the gap between fragmented services and a more highly aggregated functional system.[10] Not only are they present in the transportation field, but shadow networks exist in an uncommon stage in the reorganization of companies and in the passage of one government administration to another.

A shadow network provides for smoothness of transition. It helps in dealing with the uncertainties inherent in the design of larger functional systems. The shadow networks are a step towards a highly aggregated functional system. Our national system for health, welfare, and employment, for example, is a metasystem of shadow networks in which no one controls all the essential elements. There are multiple roots as in the building industry. Each component has a multiple constituency and vested interest exists among the providers and other related beneficiaries.

As Schön says, "Informal networks have long served to enable people to get things done when formal networks failed." The Russian *tolkatch* was created through its own personal, informal relationships of exchange between units of Soviet industry. Functioning illegally, the *tolkatch* compensates for errors in planning and has enabled industrial systems to work which would otherwise have been hopelessly paralyzed.

All large organizations have their interpersonal networks for exchanging favors on which much business depends. The very life of social systems has been dependent on the operation of informal networks.

Ad hoc networks come into being to compensate for mismatches between the institutional plan and the problems perceived as important. Informal networks go to work when there is a problem in poor communities and provide care for the sick and the young. With the loss of the stable state, Schön notes that "ad hoc networks become a permanent rather than an interim expedient. They begin to occupy a place in the foreground."[11]

Schön describes the various network roles which are essential to the design, creation, and functioning of both ad hoc and continuing networks. These roles include the systems negotiator, the underground manager, the maneuverer, the broker, the network manager, and the facilitator.

People who play network roles frequently occupy places in several subsystems. They have various organizational identities and exist on the margin of institutions. They are in effect marginal persons. This has a negative connotation of not being central and a positive connotation of being at the forefront.

At present, there are no regular setups for learning how to play network roles—at least, not for those in management. Still, there is a demand for developing learning systems and network roles to bypass internal strictures. This is where the opportunity comes for applying the tenets of networking as an overlay to the bureaucratic, hierarchical system.

NETWORK OVERLAYS

In a network overlay, communications flow throughout the network in all directions with feedback loops operating both locally and over the entire system. The network lines of communication joining the Defense Intelligence Agency (DIA) and the military services are more travelled than the lines joining different services directly with each other. DIA becomes a node in a larger network which includes the Office of the Secretary of Defense and the Service R&D organizations.

The overlay network gives form and legitimacy to those parts of the informal organization which exists in every rigidly formal system. Use of an overlay permits a manager to realize the advantages of a network mode while still maintaining the strengths of a bureaucratic organization. What this means is that administrators who participate in a network overlay require different orientations than their counterparts in a purely hierarchical, bureaucratic organization. The care and feeding of the network requires managers to shift their focus from directing and controlling to supporting. The objective is to facilitate the operations of the network and create an environment where it can flourish.

The network overlay concept is actually being applied to large bureaucracies to help them do things better.[12] The Department of Defense (DOD) has a universal reputation as a rigidly hierarchical organization. Along with the Armed Services, it is cited as a classical model of bureaucracy. Despite this fact, using a network overlay is an innovative management approach in the defense system acquisition process.

A bit of history is relevant. The network model overlaid on the formal bureaucratic structure provides meaningful intelligence support for the defense system acquisition process. Traditionally, intelligence has been treated as an appendage, perhaps an afterthought, after a program was mature and robust. A program manager was responsible for the intelligence about any threat system which might jeopardize a project, budget, or time frame. Credit for an effective job did not encourage him or her to pay much attention to a potential adversary. Congressional questioning, the shortening cycle of defense systems, the emphasis on the impact of intelligence in the system acquisition process forced the DOD to consider how intelligence could play a greater role in the weapons acquisition process. One school of thought—the antiparochials—argued that threats to all DOD programs should be produced by an independent intelligence agency. The traditional "center-periphery overlay"—have a separate defense intelligence agency (the DIA) report all programs—was the dominant model for diffusing, coordinating, and directing the efforts of dispersed elements of a large organization. Those opposed to this idea noted that the services possess competent intelligence organizations and know best the relevance of any threat to their developing systems. Therefore, intelligence gathering should remain decentralized.

The network overlay was an alternate concept introduced to exchange information, expedite the process, and learn. This concept accepts the notion that a network is a set of elements related to one another through multiple interconnections. The network mode, the center, shifts, and the leadership are ad hoc. The system network overlay determines the limits of analysis.

MARKET NETWORKS

In the Western Sahara and Sudanese precapitalist-industrialist societies, the economic function and organization of long-distance trade were, for the most part, embedded in a social organization. There existed semi-permanent market networks which corresponded to the areas under de facto control of a dominant ethnic group or state. Powerful merchants administered these trading networks, and their representatives worked together on the basis of their ethnic ties.

A more recent appearance of market networking has been evident as the traditional skills and values governing industrial growth since World War II have largely outlived their usefulness. The nature of market competition has changed and two critical skills are in the forefront: technological change and global network management in the world marketplace. Once the market networks are in place, the planned introduction, renovation, and obsolescence of key competitive technologies can occur in a given market. This is called technology cascading in a market network.

Global market network management is a systematic approach to accessing and cultivating worldwide markets while limiting the costs and risks associated with traditional ownership of foreign entities. The global market networks focus on orchestrating—not necessarily owning and controlling—global resources. Market network management may involve overseas joint ventures of less than 50 percent equity which would permit access to both open- and closed-border markets. Production and marketing arrangements can be made where one party gains market access with little or no increase in assets, while the other party earns manufacturing fees and licensing. Some schemes, where permissible, allow competitors to share excess capacity or a consortium of international competitors to join forces in a third market. Apple Computer owns 49 percent of a joint venture with Grupo Manzana in Mexico, with Manzana, having responsibility for marketing all Apple exports to Latin America. Compound market network linkages, leveraging both process and product technology to joint advantage, are indicated by the Hercules, Inc., joint production venture in California with Sumitomo Chemical Company, using polyacrylonitrile manufacturing technology developed in Japan in an earlier Sumika-Hercules venture.

In the 1960's and 1970's Monsanto Company established a market and manufacturing network of eighty-nine subsidiaries, associates, and affiliates around the world. The market network process involved many varieties of ownership, management, research and development efforts, and marketing arrangements. My role on the executive committee and board of directors of Monsanto was that of housemother to orchestrate this global network.

The key to success was having nationals of the various countries serve in responsible decision-making positions and be resident in the overseas regions. The staff at the headquarters in St. Louis, in turn, provided trust and support for the international marketing of a wide variety of products. With sales offices and agents scattered worldwide, the task of developing individual networking relationships was formidable. But, the delegation of authority and frequent meetings at headquarters and in the field kept the network personal and effective.

ROMANTIC NETWORKS

Human or social networking may reach its zenith in the romantic network. The persistent success of lonely hearts clubs, singles bars, pen pal networks, and all sorts of promotional efforts with products, happenings, and leisure activities, highlight the importance of romantic networks and the extent to which they can bring people together.

Studies of 94 male and 99 female undergraduates conducted at the University of Washington in Seattle during 1983 helped investigators develop a hypothesis linking network involvement to romantic involvement.[13] Subjects surveyed were involved in premarital heterosexual relationships. The investigators showed that this romantic involvement (unromantically called "dyadic involvement") was positively associated with perceived support of the individual's own network of family and friends, and also with the perceived support of the partner's network. The attraction to the partner's network and communication of the individual with his or her partner's network also related to the number of people actually met in the partner's network. The Romeo and Juliet effect only occurred in one sector of the network, and then for only certain variables.

The predominant relationship between social support and romantic involvement was both positive and lineal. In common sense terms, this means "get to know your prospective spouse's family."

WOMEN'S NETWORKS

Tim Heald, in *Networks*, describes the formation of new girl networks (NGN) to rival the British old boy networks (OBN) which women have so far not been able to penetrate in the United Kingdom, despite the formal acceptance of women and the beachhead established in professional, commercial, and political life. In Britain, "Network" was started by Irene Harris, who earns her living by organizing fundraising events, most notably the annual Woman of the Year luncheon at the Savoy Hotel. Ms. Harris even offers a "Network" rate at various hotels, wine merchants, and health hydros.

The expansion of women's networks has been in North America. Mary Scott Welch has documented the history of women's network movements and has developed a guide for would-be women networks.[14] One of the oldest and most successful women's networks in the United States is a women's employee group at the Equitable Life Assurance Society headquarters in New York City. Alma Novak, founder of "Networks," devised a self-help program for women so they could discuss their career problems, share information, and offer each other support. The network operates in two ways—a monthly luncheon with speakers and small, bi-weekly discussion groups.

In 1982, the National Association for Female Executives (New York) reported that about 650 women's networks were emerging each year. All sorts of variations of network functions are involved. Shelly Galehouse King has a network clearing house to match up, by computer, subscribers who can help each other. One spontaneous network focuses on research into the process of networking. Although it appears to be a one-person crusade at the present time, it is indicative of the zeal and interest in the subject of networks and networking.

Pat Underhill, editor of *Anet Paradox*, is an example of a network activist. She has launched a search for more networking information via a "noteletter." *Anet Paradox* is several years old and represents a grass roots search devoted to theories and techniques of decentralized networking. A noteletter is "sent only in exchange, 'info for info' (published or unpublished), no subscriptions, publishing or reprinting welcome." I mention this noteletter under Women's Networks, not because its target audience is confined to women, but for its casual prose which has a women-to-women oriented appeal, e.g., "altho that network coordinator's supposed purpose is to serve the members, the more time she devotes to her job, and the more expertise she develops, the less she will have in common with most members, the more her interest will diverge from theirs, and the greater her temptation to use her position for personal aggrandizement or to promote pet schemes."

The prime notion of *Anet Paradox* seems to focus around the editor's classification of two forms of people networks: a *cenet* (*ce* for centric flow and central control) which has a central office or coordinator who receives information from various sources and distributes it to members, clients, readers, and an *anet* (*a* for acentric, also for amorphous or anarchic) which has no central control! All members or participants may communicate with all others (though some may have more links than others). While this is hardly an original concept, the "paradox" seems to be that the editor's effort is directed towards *anets* yet she herself forms a *cenet*, to use Pat Underhill's vocabulary.

This chapter began with the bureaucratic bypass and suggested that the only thing that saves us from bureaucracies in the long run is their inefficiency. A more immediate relief from the red-tape worm is networking. It is the antidote to hierarchy and a process for bypassing government of some of the people, by some of the people, for some of the people. Networks can cope effectively with the people who put in their place the people who put them in their places. The message is that of Professor Raiffa: "We have to aspire higher . . . organize . . . internal infrastructures to encourage more collaborative networking."

Chapter 6

Netcom: Communications Networks, Grapevines, and Gossip

> Some are born to connections; others work
> at it . . . if architecture is frozen music,
> then social networks are frozen gossip.
> —*Paul Barker[1]*

One of my favorite cartoons shows a secretary in the executive suite speaking on the telephone saying, "I will not! You put your boss on first . . ."

Communication barriers like these have existed ever since Adam had his first misunderstanding with Eve. This was well before Petroff's twenty-seventh law of hierarchical behavior: Humility decreases with every promotion and disappears completely at the vice presidential level.[2] The secretary in the cartoon is protecting her boss from having to wait while, at the same time, asserting her gatekeeping role in the communications chain. The human element still dominates in the information age.

Within any organization or communications network people can play any of three key roles: (1) gatekeepers who, like the secretary, screen people and messages and control accessibility of information; (2) trendsetters, the opinion leaders in a network, those to whom people listen and those that influence morale and outlook of the group in which they take part; and (3) boundary-spanners, people in a network who see to it that there is information exchange or "ventilation" between an operation and its external environment. Managers who recognize these three key roles and support them enhance the effectiveness of any formal communications network.

INFORMATION TECHNOLOGY

Electronic communication technology has brought us rapidly along the path toward a truly automated office and factory where integrated information processing is a reality. If we map the information products and services available on a two-dimensional matrix according to communications responsiveness and information content, the universe of products and services looks like figures 6.1 and 6.2.[3]

The position of the basic telephone networks is at a high interactive level of communications responsiveness with relatively limited information content value added. The office grapevine, the "jungle

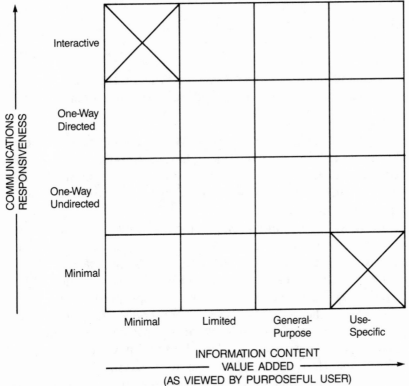

FIGURE 6.1: Axes for "map" of information products and services.

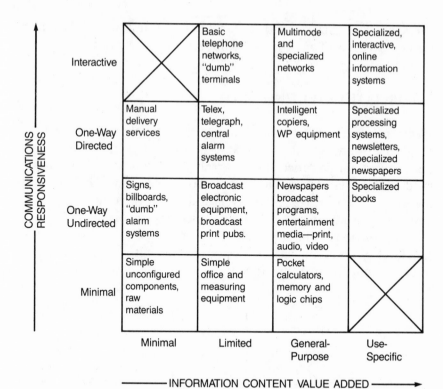

COMMUNICATIONS RESPONSIVENESS		Minimal	Limited	General-Purpose	Use-Specific
	Interactive		Basic telephone networks, "dumb" terminals	Multimode and specialized networks	Specialized, interactive, online information systems
	One-Way Directed	Manual delivery services	Telex, telegraph, central alarm systems	Intelligent copiers, WP equipment	Specialized processing systems, newsletters, specialized newspapers
	One-Way Undirected	Signs, billboards, "dumb" alarm systems	Broadcast electronic equipment, broadcast print pubs.	Newspapers broadcast programs, entertainment media—print, audio, video	Specialized books
	Minimal	Simple unconfigured components, raw materials	Simple office and measuring equipment	Pocket calculators, memory and logic chips	

←——— INFORMATION CONTENT VALUE ADDED ———→

FIGURE 6.2: Map of information products and services, example entries.

telegraph," and the gossip channels can exist in most any of the cells in the matrix. They probably belong best in the interactive level of responsiveness. Here they can range anywhere from minimal to use-specific in information content depending on how urgent or juicy the information is.

Information technology, particularly computer and data communications, can multiply the effectiveness of a decentralized human network in speed, capacity, and accuracy. Some examples are: (1) members of some real estate franchised chains and relocation cooperatives can now electronically transmit property listings from a broker in another city; (2) reservation services for independently owned hotel and rental franchises can be provided electronically; (3) in the teletype era we used to "wire flowers," now we "telebouquet" them through electronic computer communication networks.[4]

There are electronic networks whose sole purpose is communication itself. One national telephone system now has many vendors who offer different kinds of powerful internal networks. Telephones in automobiles and aircraft, and wireless telephones, which can be carried about on one's person, are readily available.

About 500 organizations in the United States sell information electronically over telephone lines to terminals or communicating personal computers. Thousands of data base provider organizations sell their information. This information services industry is well over the $2 billion annual revenue level.

Local area networks (LAN's) are communications networks which run intraoffice or interoffice if buildings are in close proximity, say up to a few miles. LAN's are characterized by their technology, transmission method, medium, network access, and interfaces. These set down physical and logical requirements that devices meet in order to connect to the network. Companies, such as, Xerox, Wang, Amdox, Sytek, Comtel Information Systems, and over sixty others, have been introducing LAN's since 1979. The biggies, IBM, AT&T, and others, have already or are expected to enter this growth market shortly.

Personal computer work stations—office automation—hooked into a unified system have been, until recently, the province of large companies that could afford them. Inexpensive computers and LAN's now allow smaller companies to install office automation on a piece-by-piece basis at a low cost and less risk. As *Fortune* writer Bro Uttal put it: "The day is finally in sight when personal computer networks will indeed approach the status of mayonnaise—holding everything together, but noticeable in themselves only for smoothness."[5]

Electronic communication isn't confined to office automation. It has invaded the classroom. As an alternative to attending classes, TeleLearning Systems of San Francisco, California, offers a new way to further one's education through an "electronics university." Courses can be taken at home by way of a personal computer and modem (a connection device between telephone and computer). TeleLearning has 170 courses of its own and also sells its network service to the military, corporations, and schools, allowing them to develop their in-house courses for use on it. The cost of a course ranges from $35 to $150 and the choices include individual tutoring programs, SAT (college entrance exams) test preparation, college level classes, and professional test preparation courses.

In the summer of 1984, the Violent Criminal Apprehension Program (VICAP) began operating at the Federal Bureau of Investigation Academy in Quantico, Virginia. Police Departments now send Quantico standardized reports on murders in their communities and certain kinds of violent assaults in which the victims survive. The data is entered into a computer and homicide specialists look for common threads. This new information network is expected to help police link "serial" killings.

ELECTRONIC MAIL

An increasing number of personal computer owners and word processor users are using their computers for daily communications with other individuals and groups. Using a personal computer to exchange messages with others is called "electronic mail." Playing post office with your electronic mailbox is easy and fun. The user deposits (types) a message addressed to another user into a control computer. That message is stored until the addressee identifies himself or herself and asks to see his or her messages. The key feature of the system is message storage. It's sort of like a telephone answering machine except that it is a visual rather than an audible way to store a message. Because the message is stored, the sender and the recipient of the message do not have to be connected to the system at the same time.

The first electronic mail system came into being when an operator of an early computer system left a note in a file for another user to read later. It was apparent such files could be "exchanged" between two users on such a system. The first application, the exchange, involved a central computer in a building that had other users in the building wired to it. Later, telephone lines, coaxial cables, microwave and satellite links were used. Eventually high-speed-packet-switching data networks were created for computers to communicate with each other, and they were opened for public dial-in use. Worldwide electronic mail was created.

There are several forms of electronic mail available. Software can turn a personal microcomputer into an electronic bulletin board. Using one's own terminal or microcomputer, anyone who has the same number can call in and connect to the bulletin board. OMNET, Inc., of Boston offers two networks: SCIENCEnet, an R&D community network, and BUSINESSnet, a business network. These offer high quality, sophisticated electronic-mail service which encourages intergroup and interdisciplinary communications. The exchange of information is either private or public, e.g., bulletin board messaging.

The Cheswick Center of Boston, a not-for-profit educational trust dedicated to the improvement of human-services institutions, has an experimental network for use in its project work. By collaborating on an electronic mail system, trustees, associates, and others can "message" back and forth on topics or projects of common interest without having to assemble physically or coordinate communication times. The messages are stored and retrieved at the pleasure of the sender and receiver. This feature is especially effective among the volunteer members of The Cheswick Center who episodically cooperate on the Center's activities, and do so from far-flung geographical locations.

Computer conferencing, or teleconferencing, is a system for linking people together using personal computers, communication technology, and conference software. Office or home terminals are linked through telephone lines to communications satellites and into a central computer. Messages to all participants are displayed on video screens and may be reproduced in hand copy on a printer. Participants can take or add messages at their own convenience, a significant difference from "real time" audio or video conferencing. Teleconferencing also differs from electronic mail in that the software facilitates group dialogue via message storing, search and retrieval, editing, cross-referencing, and report writing.

A good example of this networking by computer was C. Jackson Grayson, Jr.'s organization of a White House Conference on productivity. Dr. Grayson is chairman of the American Productivity Center in Houston, Texas, and was asked to gather the best thinking of leaders from business, labor, academia, government, and nonprofit institutions on the subject of improving productivity. Via the Electronic Information Exchange Systems (EIES) at the New Jersey Institute of Technology, 175 participants were organized into seven computerized conferences: cooperation in the work place, health care, information workers, quality, reward systems, technology, and training. Very few of the conferees had prior experience with a computer. The conference system was "on-line" seven days a week for twenty-three hours per day. Some conferees signed on three or four times a day, some several times a week. Each conference had a moderator to guide and direct the discussion. Although 95 percent of the activity took place over the electronic network from computer terminals, the moderators did meet once in Houston to assess progress. In 100 days of electronic dialogue, the seven conferences generated 2,170 conference comments, 12,700 private messages, and 177,335 lines of communication, all of which were condensed into a 150-page report.[6]

Another teleconferencing service, Participate, is among the 1,000-plus data services offered by The Source, the nation's largest "information utility," located in McLean, Virginia.

Teletraining, a natural extension of teleconferencing, is the delivery of training programs by an instructor in a central location to students in one or more remote sites. Honeywell Information Systems and the Travelers Insurance Company are examples of companies using teletraining to significantly enhance their training capabilities while simultaneously reducing training costs. A multitude of audiographics services and equipment at each site enables the instructor and students to share questions, answers, and opinions. During an eighteen-month period in 1982 and 1983, AT&T realized savings of $121,000 through teletraining.

The *Futurist*, June 1984, put together a "Networking Sampler" to identify typical network services by their primary orientation. Metanetworks are those networks which exist to network other networks. The Networking Institute, of West Newton, Massachusetts, endeavors to service the entire networking universe. Members have an everexpanding directory to over 2,000 networks and receive a networking newsletter.

The Metasystems Design Group, of Arlington, Virginia, is a computer-linked "Meta-Net" of transformationally oriented futurists.

Microcomputer Information Support Tools (MIST), of Lake Oswego, Oregon, is an integrated software package company enabling over a half dozen networking capabilities to be linked to other computers and computer conferencing systems.

Thousands of networks fit the category of information, resource, and service exchange networks. The Transnational Network for Appropriate/Alternative Technologies (TRANET), of Rangeley, Maine, is a planetary clearinghouse and resource matchmaker for thousands of organizations and individuals worldwide.

The Institute for the Information Society is one of many Japanese organizations that cooperate with the government's Economic Planning Agency to implement networking in Japan.

Citizens diplomacy took a significant step forward on August 5, 1984, when social activists in the United States, Canada, Europe, and the Soviet Union were linked through a network conference call heralded as "The First Global Town Meeting." The ninety-minute satellite broadcast produced by U.S. Radio, Inc., featured a progress report of groups and individuals working for a world beyond war.

International cooperation in agricultural research is not new but the current extent of collaboration is unprecedented. Scientists are forging working partnerships on a regional or global scale to cut costs, avoid duplicate research, and accelerate transfer of technology to farmers. The Philippines-based International Rice Research (IRR), and the International Maize and Wheat Improvement Center (*CIMMYT: Centro International de Mejoramiento de Maiz y Trigo*) in Mexico have relied on extensive networks for over twenty years and are role models for more recent networks.

Many networks exist as transformational networks with one of their purposes being the transformation of individuals and society. Examples of these are the Communications Era Task Force, located in Spokane, Washington. It sets forth actionable hopes, values, and visions of a community renewal network in the northwestern United States and southwestern Canada. The TWG Energy Field, of Arlington, Virginia, is an informal association of over 600 people interested in the dynamics of second-order institutional change, i.e., change of organizational structures rather than change within them. These last two transformational network examples are more the social network type rather than the electronic type.

Given all the advanced information technology, we tend to forget the value of social networking, the informal gossip channels, and verbal and written grapevines that persist in all organizations like crabgrass in a well-trimmed lawn. Stamping out these informal channels is not possible, nor should it be a goal. Actually, grapevines can provide a check and balance on poorly conceived plans, the rise of favoritism, and emotional situations and decisions. Grapevines provide management with uncontrolled feedback about the climate, morale, and social health of the firm, and about what is really happening in the organization.

The employee grapevine should be harvested continually and particularly during periods of excitement, change, and insecurity. Grapevines flourish whenever a firm's communication policy and practice are not in good shape, when there is little company news, and formal communications channels are too rigid or adhered to too narrowly. Wise managers know which individuals serve as grapevine links and can assist them in influencing the direction of informal communications which supplement the formal channels. It's like side communication in a boardroom. If you whisper something to your neighbor, the message gets undue attention.

Chapter 7

The Process of Networking

> Behind every individual closes
> organization; before him opens liberty.
> —*Emerson*

The maxim "When all else fails, reorganize" has reached a plateau in its usefulness. Institutions—big corporations, in particular—have attained such size and complexity that reshuffling role relationships and responsibilities often fails to increase organizational effectiveness. It has been observed that industrial cultures are dangerously overdifferentiated and underintegrated.

Spin-offs, divestments, employee buyouts, decentralization, restructuring under holding company umbrellas, and portfolio investment clusters are popular reorganizing structural variables. All this organizational geometry preserves the classical hierarchy in some form, even though it may be reductive, diminutive, compartmentalizing, or flatter in a pyramidal sense. "Let all things be done decently and in order" (I Corinthians XIV, 40) is the prevailing idea.

In comparison, the relatively disorderly movement of social networks is the secret to new organizational geometry, to getting things done in spite of the establishment. Individual members of big organizations seek liberation of their personal aspirations, beliefs, and expectations by forming human networks that go beyond their personal "ego" linkages. The reason is that human networks listen when the Orwellian establishment fails to hear.

If you are unhappily situated in an unresponsive bureaucracy, at the middle or bottom of an organizational pyramid, try extending your personal network, first within and around the hierarchy, then reach outside the boundaries of the corporation to seek kindred souls who will share your interests, concerns, or enlightenment. You can do this "professionally" without any disloyal conduct, conflict, or diversion of significant interest from the system of the firm. But you may need some lessons in this new social geometry.

Ludwig von Bertalanffy, Viennese professor of biology, founded the Society for the Advancement of General Systems Theory, in Canada, before he died in 1971. According to Bertalanffy, one of mankind's tragedies is that we have more values for complex organizations and systems than for personal conduct. This imbalance dooms the individual's morality because we are inescapably dependent on context. It is this failure to comprehend systems that has made our society disordered and antagonistic.[1]

THE SEARCH FOR NEW SOCIAL GEOMETRY

Kurt Lewin, originally a psychology professor at the University of Berlin, brought his "field theorist" approach to psychology to the United States in 1933. Before he died in 1947, he made a significant impact on organizational theory. His work centered around the belief that the psychological fields which join the personality to its life space, or immediate environment, and the life space to the larger environment beyond, were strong enough to alter the meaning of "facts." Different people could vary totally in their response to identical facts.

Lewin's seminal work on the process of organizational change, in his terms of unfreeze/change/refreeze, corresponds to the equilibrium/tension/reequilibrium formula that is central to his theory of personality growth and envelops the search for new social geometry . . . new theoretical figures in space.[2]

Our search for networking geometry is an indirect, "around end" approach to organizational effectiveness. This approach is aimed at supplementing (or replacing) conventional hierarchic and bureaucratic conduct with the conduct or influence of internal and external human networks. The networks function as underlays or overlays to the existing organizational structure. They form meaningful linkages between the life space of individuals. I perceive four stages in the search for this new geometry or sociogram of networking.

Stage One: The Ambition-Driven First Initiative

An isolated person who becomes willing and has the urge to share a hope, an idea, a problem, or an innovation may originate this type of social advance or movement. An unintentional, informal "larval" network of dispersed persons who know others, makes contact on a nonprearranged basis. The scene is one where the initiator says in effect, "Gather around, I have a message . . ." If this friendship or advice-giving exchange creates a strong common concern, an informal, intentional fledgling association is created. It is the seed or germ or a "pupal stage" human network. (See Chapter 2.)

This "I have a message . . ." initiative probably has its roots in the concept of ego-identity introduced by psychiatrist Erik Erikson. Scholars tell us that a sequence of responses to environment exhibits the virtues of each stage of the human life cycle. The sequence starts with hope, will, purpose, competence and moves on through fidelity, love, care, to wisdom of adulthood at the final stage of our life cycle. Erikson's psychoanalysis becomes a positive, ethical science where the ego holds in synthesis the virtues of these eight stages.[3] This notion is sort of the DNA of networking. The "I have a message . . ." initiative emerges at the stage where an individual has a purpose in mind. The message announces the purpose.

Stage Two: Change-Directed Action

Cooperation rather than competition symbolizes any action. Kurt Lewin's concept of life space personality linkages between individuals and the environment helps explain. Small groups of like-minded persons "retreat" from their normal environment. They gather together, literally, or in some commemorative sense, as *cliques* to incubate the will, strength, and social support required to struggle effectively for a world of new organizational arrangements. This new "geometry" of relationships is a world where every person is sovereign of his or her own life space and has access to the liberty from organization that Emerson wrote about.

A formulation of shared values and a better focus on goals starts to take place in response to the original invitation, "Gather around, I have a message . . ." The small group searches for commonly shared reasons for bringing up the notion of gathering together in the first place. This search continues without boundary. It may fragment, cluster, or string itself out in branch, chain, web, or other form with either strong, weak, or transient ties between individuals.

Stage Three: Condition-Driven Choices

The existing working or life environment may or may not be sufficiently conducive to change and satisfy the newly shared values or interests. Conditions may be such that it becomes necessary to seek personal satisfaction far outside the boundary of the institution in which the stirrings of social concern or advance are taking place. Interorganizational, as well as interpersonal, linkages can be built outside if internal conditions force external networking.

Within very large corporate organizations, informal, suborganizational linkages may also form amidst the functional or strategic unit structures. These may exist as an overlay, underlay, or shadow network of human linkages. Networks naturally coexist with other organizational structures.

The interested, mutually sharing clique (or cliques) picks an opportunity space (wherever conditions are hospitable) within or without the system boundary of their parent organization. This opportunity space offers the liberty to pursue the purpose and objectives of the change-directed action. A human network is born.

Stage Four: Focus and Formulation of a Network

Some of these new organizational relationships are useful. They usually occur in a different geometrical pattern than the relationships present in conventional structures. A network of linkages, affinities, and human associations is founded even though it may be fragile and unstable.

Generally, these human networks are open systems rather than closed systems. According to scholars, the geometry may be seen to resemble Cuvierian structural notions of the zoological vertebrata, mollusca, articulata or radiata, or the reticulated, weblike appearance of a fishnet, mobile, or spiderweb. The geometrical variations are limitless. You can form your own network to suit your fancy and the conditions encountered.

NETWORKS IN ACTION

Let's mentally walk through these four stages, in search of a new geometry of social and organizational relationships.

The Situation

The situation in many large organizations finds the individual surrounded by a series of complex, overlapping, formal, and informal environments. His or her sovereign life space is hemmed in, threatened, and confining. (See fig. 7.1.) Given the typical closed system of

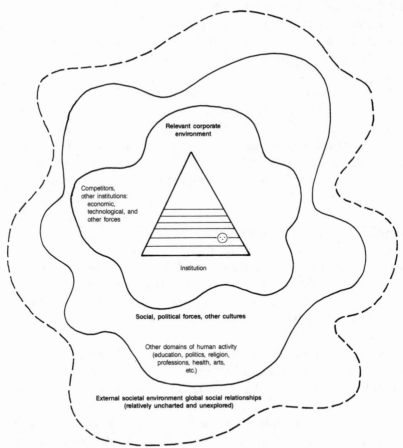

Relevant corporate
environment

Competitors,
other institutions:
economic,
technological, and
other forces

Institution

Social, political forces, other cultures

Other domains of human activity
(education, politics, religion,
professions, health, arts,
etc.)

External societal environment global social relationships
(relatively uncharted and unexplored)

FIGURE 7.1: Environmental context.

a large organization, we can also visualize the social context for an individual. One way to do this is to follow the map of overlapping boundaries of social context in which (and from which) networks may emerge. (See fig. 7.2.)

The Process

In the beginning, the initiator sends out a plea. Some casual interest develops within the organization, but nothing really happens. Employees are always giving messages. It's normal that there are rumors; gossiping takes place at the water cooler, in the cafeteria, in the john, over the telephone, via the bulletin boards or graffiti. The initiator then finds an especially concerned individual and pairs up with him or her. An alliance is formed (Stage One). These dyads, or bi-

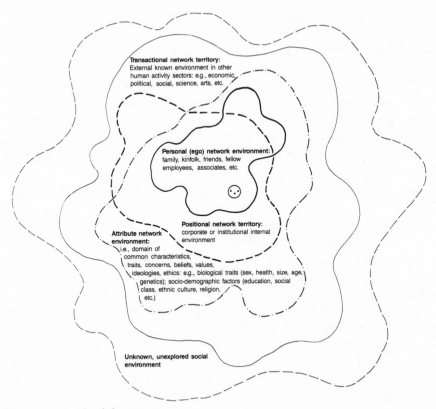

FIGURE 7.2: Social context.

nary associations, may form anywhere in an organization or between organizations. Here are some examples:

- *Director dyad.* A great deal of attention has been given to the controversial subject of director interlock and the "cooperative corporate actor networks" wherein one individual serves on two or more corporate boards simultaneously. Nearly seventy years ago, Supreme Court Justice Louis Brandeis called them "undemocratic" and a "practice of many evils." He argued that they tend to promote collusion between companies and diminish competition in the marketplace. This director dyad (or triad, etc.) phenomenon is a subject in itself. It is perhaps one of the best-known forms of networking in our business society.[4]

- *Top management dyad*

- *Mid-management dyad*

- *Underarchy (worker) dyad*

These dyads, triads, or other multiple relationships can extend themselves in various classical types of network structures.

The next network formulation step is when the original binary relationship generates a pattern of "confidant, leader, and minions."[5] This geometry can progress to a point where it may be characterized as "confidant, leader, and colleagues." The "minions" begin to share and communicate directly with each other without going through the leader. The association becomes collegial and the nature of the network may be one of friendship or advice or both (Stage Two).

The leader or a surrogate identifies an interested individual (an isolate) not in the group, and perhaps not even in the same corporate or institutional system. He or she interlocks on a personal friendship or advice basis. This newly associated isolate, as well as others in the network, utilize their ego networks or their positional networks to radiate and extend the connections. Soon other cliques form randomly within and without this growing, interlaced hook-up of shared concerns or interests. The cliques then form liaisons, variously called crony, exclusive sets, or coteries. The cognoscente chat and liaise with their friends and advisors and radiate further interconnections of either a high or low level of communication.

With such a clique formation, multiple consensus is formed. The clique becomes related even though the points of view may vary to some extent. This interlocking of cliques may be the means of bringing communications and relationships between other organizations. The bridge connector is termed a *cosmopolite*, that is, it belongs to most parts of the world.

If an individual in a communications network controls the messages flowing through a communications channel, the individual is dubbed a *gatekeeper*. An individual who interpersonally connects two or more cliques within a system, without belonging to any clique, is referred to as a *liaison*.

The clique may be formed in another institution, or perhaps, it may institutionalize itself into a unit or system of its own with a definable boundary (Stage Three). For example, the spontaneous formation of chapters of the National Association of Corporate Directors, which was started in 1984 as interest in corporate governance spread throughout the United States. The parent association, headquartered in Washington, D.C., encouraged the formation of new chapters. They came about in response to members' needs to exchange views and learn in a local scene, rather than depend solely on national or regional conferences, workshops, or written forms of headquarters' communications.

Another developmental stage in networking may occur if and when cliques liaise between each other (Stage Four). Another system or subsystem may be created with a focus on the new network's objectives. The network subsystem (if it survives) has a strong consensus and develops a life and culture of its own.

Conditions may drive the choice of further network growth in different directions. If the network becomes predominantly interorganizational in its linkage, the geometry of federation formation may evolve. Drawing from some scholarly analysis, we can depict the theoretical forms in space using figures 7.3a, 3b, 3c and 3d.[6]

There is a wide range of potential geometrical patterns. The network linkages between individuals and between organizations exist whether we wish to reorganize them or not. If we try to oversupport or overstress networks at the expense of the existing conventional structures, we run the risk of destroying the human or social network. It's like love, humor, or sex. Overanalysis or institutionalizing destroys the delicate relationships.

Networks are an ingenious way to obtain individual liberty without individual responsibility. Our elementary geometry lesson should end with the reminder that networks may or may not be the answer. Merely because we have a human network in action, or in formation,

A

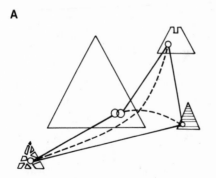

Coalition type of federation between
organizations. One has morale problems,
another has a management succession
crisis, and a third is over-regimented.

B

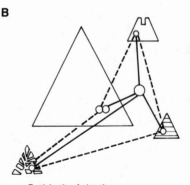

Participative federation
with self-sufficient center
acting as common communicator.

C

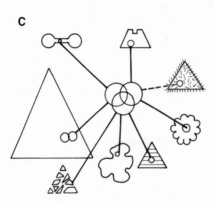

Advisory board (somewhat
ambiguous role) or peer review
group with fuzzy interpersonal
relations.

Independent federation network, with a third party
monitoring activities and decisions of the affiliates.
The central Venn-type organization connector acts
as control and is made up of three constituencies:
business, social, and government.

D

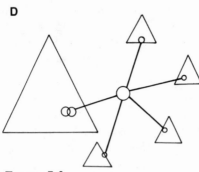

Mandated federation network, e.g., professional
sports leagues, political agencies, arbitration system.
All affiliates agree to relate through the central node
of "control."

FIGURE 7.3

does not mean the network is a sharing, caring one, or is on the right
course to improve the commonweal or the effectiveness of an existing
organization. We must be realistic about the new geometry. As a rear
bumper sticker reads: "You've obviously mistaken me for someone
who cares."

Chapter 8

Hi-Tech Wetenschapswinkels and Hi-Touch Centers

> In case no one has noticed a virulent new strain of organization—the "Center for"—appears to be sweeping across the nation . . .
> —K. M. Reese

Small organizations intent on focusing on social, political, technological, environmental, and consumer problems are establishing centers of interest around the world with flexible organizational structures and modest budgets. The centers act as information-collecting and disseminating nodes in networks of concerned persons with a common cause or interest. Most frequently the activity is voluntary. The centers tend to be transaction oriented and data base collectors. They are nonhierarchical, nonbureaucratic in concept and structure. In some cases the centers have no physical space but float in society, meeting or communicating via telephone, mail, or computer.

My first real encounter with this form of unorganization was on election as a trustee of The Cheswick Center. To date the principal focus of the Center has been governance function. There are no full-time employees of the Center. Many volunteers from academe, religious organizations, government, professions, and business backgrounds offer their services via an informal networking process. They volunteer and provide consulting help on projects targeted at improving the effectiveness of boards of directors of not-for-profit organizations. Various foundations and individuals fund these projects. A part-time project team is assembled from a network of available staff who convene specifically for the task at hand. The participants have other active interests and optional or regular sources of employment.

An example of a product of this Center is the booklet "The Cheswick Process: Seven Steps to a More Effective Board." This booklet was produced in 1982 as part of a three-year board development project with the Graduate Theological Union, Berkeley, California. The project was supported financially by the Lilly Endowment, and the work was conducted by The Cheswick Center and its associates. "The Cheswick Process" is a case-history-illustrated approach to developing an effective board of trustees. This is achieved by providing the governing bodies of seminaries and schools of theology with a governance education program, tools, and curriculum to make themselves more effective at governance.

The Cheswick Center is an example of what I call a hi-touch center. As such, it deals in the human side of governance matters. The issues tackled are emotional, ecclesial, political, social, philosophical, subjective, and, in many instances, symbolic. Other hi-touch centers deal with environmental, social, intellectual, educational, professional, and political movements. In Washington, D.C., eighty-five entries in the telephone directory begin with "Center for," for example, the Center for Applied Linguistics, the Center for Strategic Studies, the Center for the Study of Multiple Gestation, The Center for the Study of Moral Order, and the Center for Unique Learners.

A recent project of the Council for Basic Education, Washington, D.C., was the formation of a new network center for connecting eleven university-based institutes in nine cities in the United States. Each of the seven math institutes and four science institutes in the network is actually a union of a school district, a local college or university, and a philanthropic foundation or corporation. The council acts as a center to broker and monitor programs to retain or upgrade the skills of math and science teachers.

In my travels I have spent undue time in foreign telephone kiosks checking out the prevalence of hi-touch and hi-tech centers listed in various telephone books. Here are my findings as of late 1984.

Paris: 887 centers, for example, Centre Technique In-
                      terprofessionnel de Fruits et Legumes, Centre
                      Catholique des Japonais de Paris, Centre de For-
                      mation et d'Innovation

Brussels:	383 centers, including Centre Anti-Poisons, Centre de Therapie and de Recherche Sexologiques, there is even a Centre de Coiffeurs Calvitiens (bald people only!)
London:	33 centers, including Center for Overseas Pest Research and the Center for Research Into Adolescent Breakdown; the Westminister Reference Library has eighty books listed on the subject of "Centres for, . . ." such as, *Centre of Belief*, *Centre for Agricultural Strategy*, *Centrepoint: Guide for Young Homeless People in London*
New York:	121 centers; among the more interesting titles are Center for Advancement of Mankind, Center for Applied Esoteric Knowledge, and Center for Networking
Los Angeles:	38 centers, including Center for Innovative Speakers
Chicago:	38 centers
Boston:	36 centers
San Francisco:	24 centers
Montreal:	1 center called Center for the Whole Person! (Must be a lonely Montrealer.)

Europe is experiencing a mushrooming of hi-tech centers in particular. In many countries these are the offshoots of student rebellions of the 1960's and environmental movements of the 1970's. In certain instances these "science shops" have picked up powerful political and financial support from local and national governments.

In Holland, the "science shops" or network centers were started in the early 1970's and are called *wetenschapswinkels*. In France, *boutiques de sciences* abound and are somewhat misleading in title but have the same function of providing a center for empowering a network of persons interested, for example, in focusing more university research on social problems.

Wetenschapswinkels (WW) exist at all Dutch universities. At some there are even several specialized WW, e.g., biotechnology and electronics. They offer free information on science and technology to individuals and groups who need it and cannot afford to pay for it, such as neighborhood groups, environmental protection groups, labor action groups, etc. WW do not work for companies nor offer their services for commercial purposes. They typically have a minimal staff of part-timers (financed by the university), a core group of volunteers (mostly students), and a network of contacts who donate their time and may be reimbursed for expenses. Their origin is in the student movement of the 1960's, which also gave rise to the *wetswinkels* ("law shops") which offer legal advice to those who cannot afford legal fees.

The name "shop" was chosen because it presents a lower psychological threshold for its target clientele than "office," "center," and other business-related expressions. Therefore, "science shop" or, perhaps more accurately, "technology shop," is a good translation for *wetenschapswinkel*.

The WW came about out of public complaints that science had become excessively elitist and out of touch with social problems. The biggest science shop is at the University of Amsterdam, which created an official science shop in 1977, provided salaries for the fifteen staff members, a three-story building, and an annual budget equivalent to $50,000 for expenses. In addition, the university agreed that 15 percent of it's research budget, starting in 1986, will be devoted to science shop-type activities.

A network friend at Delft University believes that WW are not really flourishing networks except perhaps in some areas such as soil or ground water analysis for environmental action groups. He confirms that the origin of WW lies in the democratization movement of the 1960's when the technical universities felt they had to render some sort of social service to the public at large.

An offshoot of the WW networks are the so-called transfer points at the technical universities which offer technical advice to small companies that do not normally turn to research institutions or independent laboratories. In contrast to the WW, the transfer points do work for companies in support of commercial projects, charge for their services and are part of the university organization. The WW do get some financial support from the universities, but they are not part of the organization, and they are tolerated rather than encouraged. Here's another example of how networks exist along with hierarchically structured educational and research organizations.

The English counterparts to WW reflect some difference in form and emphasis. They are called alternative research centers or technology networks and are becoming known as "science shops." The objective of these centers is to provide a means for members of the public to seek answers to scientific and technical questions arising in their daily lives. The centers permit scientists and engineers to apply their training skills and knowledge to topics of social concern.

Science magazine reported on March 16, 1984, that the Amsterdam science shop received over 1,600 questions from more than 800 different groups and individuals on environment, health, housing, and working conditions. More than 20 percent of the questions required the initiation of research projects.

Many of what the French call *soixantehuitards*—which one sociologist has characterized as "moral entrepreneurs" turned "moral custodians"—see science shops as an appropriate direction in which public funds should be channeled. This means networks are receiving government support in some European countries.

Difficulties persist in Dutch, French, and English science shops include (1) getting scientists to accept that answering questions posed directly by the public should be considered a legitimate part of their professional responsibilities, (2) matching volunteer scientific networker skills with public inquiries which are often multidisciplinary, (3) finding scientists who do not seek a technological fix to complex social problems, (4) finding a scientist who will risk theoretical purity, (5) working the technology networks in, as well as against, the market (for example, disseminating the products of community-based research and development workshops that are a part of the center's network), and (6) balancing political and economic principles with technological principles.

To check up on this science shop movement, I tapped my personal European network of friends and associates in Brussels. A recent brochure from the "Wetenschapswinkel Delft" explains the situation in Holland as of January 1986. The brochure lists addresses of forty-one WW at thirteen Dutch universities and colleges. Half of them are "general" WW; the others are specialized in one or another field; chemistry, biology, pharmaceuticals, physics, environment, construction, economics, literature, and education.

- *Objectives*

  First, to make know-how available to the "underprivileged"; second "to promote socially useful orientation at the university"

- *Clientele*

  Individuals or—preferably—groups who don't have the means to get an answer to their questions elsewhere; definitely *no* commercial purpose; typically, clients are neighborhood committees, environmental groups, groups of workers

- *Modus operandi*

  The WW receives the request and decides whether it meets acceptance criteria; reformulates the request, if necessary, and tries to find someone to handle it among university staff, students, or other WW; assures follow-up and feedback

- *Examples of requests*

  Critique of a traffic plan for a neighborhood committee
  Soil analysis at the request of inhabitants of a neighborhood
  Analysis of toxic impurities in heroin at request of the Rotterdam Junkie Association
  Analysis of copypaper for workers in a printshop worried about possible presence of heavy metals

Centers for matching social and physical science research networks with political and economic problems will continue to grow despite the foregoing barriers. Similar network center projects are starting in West Germany, Belgium, Italy, Switzerland, and Australia. Hi-tech WW and hi-touch centers are here to stay. These network centers are a new means of getting things done.

Chapter 9

Successfully Managing Innovative Networks

> One person procreates a thought, a second
> carries it to be baptized, a third begets
> children by it, a fourth visits it on its
> deathbed, and a fifth buries it.
> —*G. V. von Lichtenberg, The Elder*

Poincaré was reported to have said, "Natural sciences talk about their results; the social sciences talk about their methods." And so it is with networking and innovation in the social domain and the realm of management. They are both uniquely human in character and beset with methodology-oriented academic research.

General innovation and networking theories are relatively new in the scheme of things. The process of innovation and the process of networking are both difficult to tie down in practical terms. However, this task was the keystone in a study of technological innovation done in 1963 by ADL for the National Science Foundation.[1] ADL's experience with hundreds of specific cases of technical innovation and some one hundred technical audits during the fifteen years previous to the study provided the background in five industrial areas: textiles, machine tools, construction, appliances, and semiconductors. Organizational patterns and methods, internal conflicts, stresses of management organizations, and industry characteristics were examined. It was apparent that a professional viewpoint was emerging—an innovation ethic.

Another relevant ADL study, done in 1965 for the Director of Defense Research and Engineering, was on the weapon system developments. The study concluded that for sixty-three successful information-generating events in the programs of weapon development the matter of organization and management styles was clearly a determining factor. An adaptive, flexible, networking-type culture was the one that stimulated innovations and subsequent development of new weapon systems. There were fifty-nine events in the innovation process driven by adaptive environments, three events with no key, definable driving force, one event that had only one person involved, and no innovative events that took place in an authoritative environment.

This chainlike, adaptive phenomenon of how the intellectual component of innovation behaves in the mosaic of the management process was later the subject of a nontechnical book.[2] This book addressed how to understand the network process of innovation and how to convert a company's interest in innovation into innovative action. The emphasis was on the steps of creation, discovery, development, growth, survival, innovation, and renewal. Achievement of useful change, the essence of innovation, depends on interrelationships and nonlinear networks in a human management system.

The temper of innovation is that of positive networking rather than revolutionary or rebellious. If it antagonizes and is unacceptable, by definition an innovation lapses. If, through interpersonal linkages, an innovation satisfied a want or nullifys an annoyance, as the socialists say, the innovation gathers a following and is accepted. Human networks play a key role in such acceptance.

The major problem in innovation management is that the usual organizational pattern—the hierarchical and bureaucratic structures and processes—are set up for yesterday's business. The inflexibility, the unwillingness to open up and permit needed changes, thwart innovation as the introduction of useful change. We tend to assume that values are firm and constant, and with human nature being what it is, maintenance of the establishment is often sacrosanct. It has been observed that rich farmers are the ones who make agricultural innovations; farmers who just scrape by stick to tried methods.

Networking, as the nonlinear communication and action process, is vital to the introduction of novel products and processes, and to the acceptance of culture, attitude, and mind-set changes of an organization. Unfortunately, most managers are unskilled and often unaware of the interpersonal process of networking and its potential for effecting influence and wielding power. This chapter attempts to describe the vital components of managing innovation, including the notion of human networking.

Managing innovation, with or without networking, is not a crisply defined process. There must be elbow room for serendipitous happenings. No real guidelines can be set for such events, other than the principle that the corporate attitude should be favorable to nonconformists and divergent thinking. Consider the baker in a small Florida town who was a volunteer fireman. Twenty minutes after he had placed rolls in the oven, the fire alarm sounded. Rather than let the rolls burn, he took them out, thinking they were ruined. On his return three hours later, he rebaked them instead of throwing them out. Thus he discovered brown-and-serve rolls for which General Mills paid him $400,000. The phrase "half-baked" doesn't have a bad connotation any more.

THE VENTURE ORGANIZATIONAL CONCEPT

The major barrier to important entrepreneurial innovations within the modern corporate framework is the organizational hierarchy itself. The structure and mind-set hierarchical hang-up is manifested by the inertia of the managers in power, whose tendency is often to neglect, sequester, or smother the entrepreneur or the networker. The management challenge is to open up the system to networking and unconventional thinking while still maintaining adequate control. This is a management balancing act and no rigid guidelines exist for the process.

However, large organizations have long been experimenting with this management balance. One of the most evident experimental trials has been in the new venture realm. Companies, such as, AT&T, Dow, Westinghouse, Monsanto, Dupont, E.G.&G., Bolt Beranek and Newman, Emerson Electric, 3M, and many others, have good and bad experiences to observe in this more open system approach to innovation via the venture organization route.

One insightful—if abstract—perspective on the advantages of venturing in a semiautonomous context was offered almost two decades ago by Mark Hanan.[3] Six characteristics of the organizational environment conducive to successful venturing prescribe a climate necessary for the innovation and networking processes to flourish. The new venture ambiance must be one where the participant's mind-set is unidirectional, multidisciplinary, eclectic (selective), entrepreneurial, judicious, and kinetic. The organizational culture is dedicated to change and multidimensional, free-style communication and action. This has to be balanced with some control, but also has to be purposeful and not overly constrained by hierarchical structure or bureaucracy. Networks are intrinsic to this condition.

The 3M Company is renowned for its innovations. It is less known for its dedication to the process of networking. 3M looks for "uninhabited markets" and "entrepreneurs from within." According to Robert M. Adams, director and R&D chieftain, "start little and build."

The bedrock principle of free communication within 3M is recognized in the motto: "If you need help, go find it anywhere." Two corollary principles are required: (1) know where to look for the information you need and (2) have it be made available when you ask. Many observers have put their finger on these company rules as 3M's key strengths over the years. The emphasis is on internal communications (networks) as illustrated by the well-known 3M Technical Forum, which the company established to encourage professional people to mix and exchange ideas. The Forum is an internal society network run by professionals which holds seminars on all sorts of technical topics drawn from the work going on in various company laboratories. In more recent years, it has been broadened to include management and behavioral science subjects. The essence is networking at any time or place, i.e., formal or informal communication and action.

Networking provides tremendous power to get new ideas accepted or new actions underway. Six times as much energy is required to start a flywheel from a standstill than as to keep it going once it is in motion. To start a new idea, or a change, requires six times as much power than as to keep existing activities going in traditional directions. Networks and networking can empower an organization to alter its course or accept change.

MANAGEMENT PERSPECTIVES ON INNOVATION

The survey in *Fortune* magazine's issue of January 7, 1985, of security analysts and business leaders is one of an annual series to determine the reputation of leading American companies as measured by eight attributes. Innovation is one of the most important attributes

distinguishing the leading companies within different industry segments. In addition, a company's ability to successfully manage innovation correlates with its value as a long-term investment.

As part of a research project started in 1983, ADL and its subsidiary company, Opinion Research Corporation, studied top management's view of the innovation process via a questionnaire completed
in mid-1985 by a cross-section of senior executives in the United
States, Western Europe, and Japan.[4] The findings, conclusions, and
implications are derived from 971 survey respondents, the majority
of whom were chief executive officers, managing directors, presi-
dents or chairpersons of both manufacturing and service companies.
Eleven important innovation practices and opinions were explored.
Six of these sets of findings reveal the importance of networking (or
potential for networking) in effecting an innovative management
practice. The findings are as follows:

1. Top management is becoming more dependent on innovation as
   a means to generate growth and profit.
   - Among the Japanese, two-thirds say it is becoming *"much
     more important,"* a figure considerably higher than that for
     North America or Europe.
   - Most CEO's see the need for innovation to become more acute
     within their companies, due to maturing markets and, in the
     United States, deregulation of many industries.
   - The rapid dissemination of information throughout society by
     electronic and human networks, and increased sophistication
     of worldwide distribution systems are increasing competition,
     and hence the need for innovation.

2. North American companies are less likely to have specific corporate expectations for the contribution of innovation.
   - 51 percent of North American respondents have specific cor-
     porate expectations compared with 71 percent in Europe and
     87 percent in Japan.

3. Innovation can be managed, but it requires specific skills and
   knowledge.
   - In the North American sample the likelihood that a good idea
     would be successfully implemented is only 38 percent, even
     though the majority of respondents consider themselves to be
     more innovative than their competition. Comparable numbers
     were 39 percent in Europe and, surprisingly, only 16 percent in
     Japan.

4. CEO's vary in their assessment of their roles in innovation.
- Three out of five chief executives believe that their proper role in the organization is to delegate primary responsibility for innovation to others, while retaining a leadership role.
- Only one-third think their proper role is to take a direct, active role, or to champion a particular project.
- Nearly all respondents reject the idea of fully delegating responsibility to others.
- On average, CEO's surveyed in Europe and North America spend 25 percent of their time on matters concerned with the management of innovation. Japanese CEO's spend 35 percent of their time on innovation.

5. Several barriers must be overcome if companies are to become more innovative.
- There are many barriers to innovation within a large company. The majority of executives in all countries agreed that preoccupation with existing problems and short-term problems is the single greatest barrier to innovation (81 percent in North America, 79 percent in Europe, and 53 percent in Japan).

6. There are three phases of innovation.
- The overall process of managing innovation can be broken down into three major phases: *invention*—the generation of ideas; *incubation*—the practical development of the idea; and *introduction*—the successful implementation of the idea in the external marketplace or in the internal corporate unit that will benefit.
- Management's most critical role in maximizing potential benefits during all three phases of the innovation process is to provide a climate that will promote and sustain innovative efforts. Human networks and the networking process are essential elements.

7. Creating a favorable climate is the most important single factor in encouraging innovation.
- Openness to new ideas from all levels is a requirement among other attributes.
- Although the climate differs within companies and countries, it can be measured by such factors as ability to balance short-term profits with long-term R&D investments, ability to try experiments throughout the organization, openness in communications, and several other factors which foster or charac-

terize an organization that balances hierarchical control with networking.

8. The sources of inspiration vary across cultures.
   - A major source of creative ideas in all geographic areas surveyed is input from within the organizations, particularly dedicated groups.
   - In North America other industry sources of ideas are important. In Europe, customers are a prime source as is the academic community. The Japanese profile is more European than American with even greater attention placed on the academic community.

9. Japanese executives take a broader view of innovation.
   - The Japanese respond "a great deal" to the need for innovation occurring in the following areas: product, service, marketing, production, distribution, and social dimensions of doing business. The Japaneses are more likely to recognize opportunities for innovation in these seven areas. In only an eighth area—management—do North American respondents top the Japanese in seeing the need for innovation in management (32 percent in North America, 30 percent in Japan and 27 percent in Europe).
   - This survey indicates that management should not confine innovation efforts to the product arena. Organizational communications in all functions are important.

10. New organizational mechanisms are being used to overcome traditional barriers.
    - Of the enabling mechanisms listed, task forces, individual champions, joint ventures, and acquisitions are the most frequently mentioned in the United States and Europe.
    - While the Japanese use task forces and joint ventures, they also use new business startups, partial spinoffs, supplier partnerships, and such financial mechanisms as R&D limited partnership or licensing agreements.
    - Japanese companies are less likely to use individual champions. Their group dynamics differ from those of other nationalities.

11. The creative use of compensation systems and other rewards can reinforce innovation.
    - Seven out of ten respondents use personal recognition from top management to encourage innovation.

- While it is not too difficult to motivate innovators, it is also very easy to demotivate them. Indifference, bureaucratic policy and procedures, strict hierarchical communication control are the most cited demotivators.
- Nature and importance of rewards differ widely by country. North Americans pay more attention to financial rewards while the Europeans and Japanese emphasize personal recognition and nonmonetary rewards.
- In all countries direct communication and action from the top is critical. This means utilizing a direct network link between the top executive and the innovator wherever he or she is located in the hierarchy.

The overall response rate of 16 percent to the questionnaire was surprisingly high, showing top management interest in innovation. The response rate was 20 percent in North America, 16 in Europe and 9 percent in Japan in the 5,828 questionnaires sent out worldwide.

FROM VISION TO REALITY

Another part of the ADL research project on innovation involves the question of how successfully innovative companies confront the difficulty and challenge of managing innovation. Twenty-nine companies were studied: ten in the United States, three in Canada, two in Belgium, two in France, two in the Netherlands, two in Sweden, two in the United Kingdom, two in West Germany, and four in Japan.

We learned that innovative companies are continually alert to change and that they take specific actions. They create a proper climate, stimulate the search for new ideas and opportunities, energize idea development, and motivate, reward and sustain innovators. In all four of these initiatives, organization structure networking practices is one key to success.[5]

The following excerpts and interpretations are confined to the innovation "lessons," learned from the companies studied, which involve the human networking process. Networks and networking ubiquitously appeared repeatedly in various raiment throughout the ADL worldwide research program.

Item: Increased attention to innovation is caused by several factors, the first of which is accelerated dissemination of new ideas. This acceleration is helped by information technologies and direct person-to-person communication in large organizations. It is also occurring intraorganizationally through professional society, trade association, and other industry and governmental communication channels.

Item: A new diagnostic tool, the Innovation Climate Index, provides an instrument to compare management's perceptions of the existing climate for innovation in a company with management's view of an ideal climate and the actual situation in comparable innovative companies. One of the five significant factors in a collection of over thirty attributes used in diagnosing the organizational structure, management systems, style, and values (as they impact on innovative climate) was found to be the extent of informal communications within the organization, i.e., the extent to which networks and networking were in operation. For example, a disparity in management's desire for a centralized structure with hierarchic tendencies and its desire for open communications reveals the degree of opportunity for incorporating networking to enhance innovativeness.

Item: Japanese quality and productivity circles are well known. The notion of employee discussion groups is spreading worldwide. The TRW company in the United States uses a "one-in-five" system for discussion groups. Each year 20 percent of the employees are selected to participate. One out of five persons from various organizational units create a mix across the company departments and functions. The networking groups meet frequently with the CEO or senior managers. The personnel director moderates. Networks and networking are thereby endorsed and empowered.

Item: Club Méditerranée, S.A., headquartered in Paris, provides a striking example of induced networking with its staff rotation scheme which breaks down hierarchical barriers. The managers call the practice "nomadism." The staff of each vacation village is moved every six months. In addition, managers swap jobs every two to four years. Everyone agrees that this cross-fertilization, continual formation and reformation of close human network linkages between staff members, enhances direct communication, action, and innovation. Networks and networking can be a powerful factor in management effectiveness.

Item: Medtronic, the world's largest manufacturer of implantable cardiac pacemakers, provides a good example of the power of network-type thinking. The company encourages lateral thinking among employees, i.e., by rearranging available information so that it is snapped out of the established pattern and forms a new and better pattern. Among the many ways Medtronic achieves lateral thinking is through encouragement of direct networking between staff members. Medtronic's business and technology center is laid out like a shopping mall; each new business venture is a separate "store," but the staff have ready, direct access to all the other "stores" and their personnel at all times without formal approval policies or procedures.

Item: The bottom-up approach for generating new ideas draws on employees and managers at all levels in the company. The Bromont plant of Canadian General Electric is a good example. Employees are trained to be multiskilled so that they not only contribute more to the business but are also able to spot and suggest improvements. Bromont uses an Idea Exchange Committee on Technology to review all ideas and help employees define them. The communication linkage is direct networking with those concerned, regardless of the organizational hierarchy.

Item: ASEA (Allmänna Svenska Elektriska Aktiebolaget), AB, in Sweden features an idea sponsorship program. Top management empowers five well-known senior managers to advocate and promote new ideas. Creation of these five stimulating "nodes" form a network designed to foster the bottom-up generation of new ideas.

These network and networking features of innovative company practices are an important part of the patterns identified by the ADL research. The program is continuing worldwide, adding to a data base of how to use and successfully manage innovation networks.

We have perhaps added a corollary to George Bernard Shaw's observation that "science never solves a problem without creating ten more." The corollary is that in order to successfully manage innovation in our complex, diversified, interdependent environment, from within and outside our corporations, we need to create ten (or more) networks to solve our problems.

Networkers can accumulate power and influence by control of information and learning. Personal chemistry, trust, and respect are the powerful forces of human relationships. Common response to leadership and the reciprocal outlet for personal enthusiasm and drive are enhanced by networking. Networking is normal. Therefore, innovative companies nourish the culture for positive networking. Networking is a political-social process and a source of informal power.

A network is a lot of little holes tied together with a fragile string—a chain of one-on-one linkages to enable the holes of ignorance or resistance to be filled or sealed. While we define innovation as making useful changes in a system or introducing a novel policy, product or process, the act of making a change for change sake is not always the proper course of action.

Managers can balance the bias toward systems and control with appreciation and sponsoring of networks and networking. Otherwise, nineteenth-century British preacher Charles Haddon Spurgeon's observation may prevail: "Alteration is not always improvement, as the pigeon said when it got out of the net and into the pie."

Chapter 10

Do I Network? You Can Bet Your Life I Do

I never realized how significant personal networks were in my life until one rainy day last July when worrying about how, in this book, to share with others the joy, the blues, and the rewards of networking. I reflected that my worries and desires usually can be successfully tackled if I tap my own network resources. Any low points in emotional cycles, any stalemate in my searches for problem solutions, writer's block, any yearnings for usefully linking ideas together, any pining for past associations with former colleagues or mentors, any hankering to share some triumph or insight with someone who understands and cares, any longing to learn something new or any urge to help someone in trouble . . . all of these can be served by networking, provided you have nourished your own networks over the years.

THE PERSONAL PERSPECTIVE

My networks take on a life of their own when I immerse myself in a particular network. Networks can be what we imagine them to be and what we make them. They become comforting (or troubling) social fictions shaped by and created by human interaction and perception. My person-to-person contacts generate imagery and symbols, metaphoric and otherwise, to help in the search for action, learning, sharing, exploring, or just plain enjoyment and fun.

Musing over all this after just experiencing my three-day fiftieth reunion in St. Louis, at the Washington University School of Engineering and Applied Sciences, made me think. While nostalgia "ain't what it used to be," the reenergizing of half-century-old, neglected relationships was emotionally and physically rewarding. Only seven out of fourteen of my undergraduate class of 1934 were survivors. We regaled each other with our past foibles and our subsequent career achievements.

Members of other schools at the university having their fiftieth reunions brought together diverse memories of glee club trips and quartet performances. Leo Samet, former St. Louis Symphony violinist, played for us. Tilly and Herman Warshofsky Finkelstein joined us at the dinner celebration, Fred Deming, Lou Horton, and Virgil Wodicka (several fraternity brothers) reminded me of the weak and strong bonds that were forged during Sigma Phi Epsilon pledge days.

There were many old faces and lots of new teeth. Some reunioners were frisky and full of ginger; others were relaxed and enjoying retirement. Too many were widowed, and a few were obviously not as vigorous as they might be. Many of the social contacts we had implicitly made years ago were latent but there.

The old boy networks were rekindled and served us all, and the university, in good stead. Our class gift to the school was the largest in history—albeit a small down payment on the personal connections, relationships and networks we fashioned years ago. These linkages don't die. They fade substantially but they're still there. It was like a spirit world, ready to support or comfort anyone who felt the need to rekindle the association by reconnecting where there is mutual interest or concern. The university is the mother figure in this symbolic networking sense.

Thinking further about fading personal relationships brings to mind the "severed network" condition often encountered in the course of one's career. The rapid decay of a network bond is a normal process in our mobile society. The connections least likely to be severed are those linkages in our ego networks, i.e., family, kinships, and close friendship networks.

The networks most likely to be severed are the transactional variety, where the linkage is predominantly an exchange on an explicit quid pro quo basis. Some examples are: customer, client and supplier contacts; club memberships; and legal, accounting and other professional service relationships. Attribute networks—those where the networkers have some attribute or interest in common, such as, religion, music, social cause, professional association, old school tie, even a geographical-neighborhood association—often become latent linkages or are severed by neglect.

Positional linkages nourished by a functional or superior-subordinate relationship in a hierarchy can decay quite rapidly when there is a change in power flow. I was surprised during two significant career changes—first, from Sinclair Refining Company to Monsanto Company, then to Arthur D. Little—to observe those with whom I had close positional bonds elect to either retain or scuttle any affinity or personal relationship after my role changes. Older and wiser now, I realize the power of position in a networking sense and the worth of personal trust and friendship which endures a political reconfiguration of relations.

THE PROFESSIONAL PERSPECTIVE

In talking my reflections over with several professional colleagues who were into organizational and behavioral consulting and educated in the soft sciences, I realized that my belated insight into human interactions was old hat to those scholars who know about social networking. Most research, however, is based on problem areas that people encounter rather than on the personal, career fulfillment sphere or management domain.

Psychologists and sociologists apply conceptual models in organizational networks to community and mental health programs dealing with alcoholism, and any activity where the relationship between social support and behavior is important. These social support networks provide counseling and deal with such topics as: stress, coronary-prone behavior, environmental modification by psychosocial rehabilitation practitioners, low-income, high-risk mothers, and parent education programs.

I had never thought of professional networking in these social domains as being relevant in process, structure, or concept to my personal networking, or to management. However, my notions of networking were advanced considerably through a series of networkshops held at ADL's Acorn Park headquarters during which fourteen associates explored networks and networking as a new way of management thinking and practice. The makeup of our multidisciplinary "networkshoppers" was interesting. Clinical psychologists, operations researchers, computer experts, MBAs, a historian, physicist, sociologist, an aeronautical engineer, a civil and chemical engineer, organic chemist, journalist, and mathematician pooled their brains to ponder how networking could help large organizations become more effective. The premise was that organization as we know it is obsolete in the information society. We delved into the idea of social networking and found out how the process functions and empowers those helping others.

Some of the things we talked about were fascinating: network social structures are created naturally by (1) the disadvantaged, (2) the illiterate, (3) those seeking strength from social networking, such as, families who provide a supportive network for deinstitutionalized mental patients. Work in Canada among undergraduate students has demonstrated the affect of friendship networks on drug users. The normative expectations of one's friends prove to be important influences.

Networks designed to help are all over the place. Three types of social support networks, tangible, emotional, and informational, develop in relation to stressful life events, psychological symptoms, morale problems and physical health status.

The social network pattern is a useful construct for analysis of social relationships. It is an instrument that seems to be used in studying and improving most human activities except, with rare exception, in management and business! Social network analysis, tried and true, is a concept leading to a description of the human relations which exist between persons. Features of a social network analysis include both structural and interactional variables. The clinical significance of social networks may be supportive or destructive. During the networkshops the question kept coming up: Why hasn't management incorporated this social service know-how into its bag of techniques and concepts of business and organizational development and administration?

We examined this line of thinking further. The skills of network management require: the ability to combine appreciation of problem structure and opportunity space with an appreciation of political structure, human resources, and the significance of symbolism in corporate culture. Opportunity space must be regarded as a scarce resource to be deployed selectively. From a behavioral standpoint, an organization can act either as a constraining or an enabling influence. Perhaps by providing appropriate supports for those organizations that have networking skills (or are capable of acquiring them), management can provide new influences which improve corporate effectiveness.

We recognize that development of network managing skills may be politically sensitive because it requires the freedom to explore alternative organizational processes. This freedom can sometimes be bought by accepting constraints on the use of sensitive information . . . a normal technique in management consulting.

But, our discussions raised the point that the use of networks seems to violate the assumptions implicit in much operations research OR theory and professional management practice. For example, conventional wisdom dictates that there be a relevant, identifiable, single decision maker in an organization. Or, it assumes that conflicts be resolved by reference to a sufficiently high authority.

We decided that the use of networking skills can bring the concepts of OR and behavioral science together. OR concepts in networking have long been recognized in many physical and technical areas, such as, communications and transportation. Networks have historically been the subject of theoretical OR, offering the techniques of topology (graphs), exploring the connectivities that can be changed unpredictably and, therefore, using methods of probability and stochastic theory to determine what will happen. Just the stuff that OR is designed to handle.

Our group recognized that this OR approach has been used to deal with such complex problems as survival of military communications systems under attack, civilian sabotage, recognizing natural forces such as earthquakes, and in scheduling transport networks. Techniques well known are critical paths and pert charts which are used, for example, in scheduling transport networks. The opportunity space for network analysis in human resource functions is a natural domain for future development.

Given an insight into a professional business opportunity to use networking in an explicit way, I realized that personal talent and skill are the key to exploring and utilizing networking. This made me think more objectively about my own networking and how to improve it.

THE IMAGE PROBLEM

Having worked in the industrial establishment for thirty-three years before going into management consulting and contract research, my value system was greatly shaped by the large company model. Hierarchy, structure, goals, formal roles and relationships, command-communication, and the central doctrine of conventional business were the norm. Management development courses, company-sponsored or outside the firm, emphasized logical decision making, rational planning, sequential operations, and quantitative measurement. Nowhere was there but a whisper about the cultural climate, texture, and symbolism which puts individual aspirations on an equal footing with focus on corporate mission or expected conduct.

I learned about networking—without calling it that—from my experience on various boards of directors, for both nonprofit and profit organizations, during this career period. Recruitment and nomination of directors was essentially via the old boy network, especially in earlier days. The mid-1970's witnessed a more objective approach in many companies to directorship selection.

My immediate family members—the distaff and daughter side—were more right-brain oriented, educated in arts and humanities, and wiser about person-to-person relationships. It was routine in their world to work and play with people and organizations oriented toward personal and spiritual growth, health and life cycles, counselling and cooperatives—all "soft" science areas. In my world, "hard" science, logic and formality, was the proper orientation for a business career.

In fact, the various organizations and subcultural movements outside my world were not considered completely respectable or important. These included Far East religious zealots, health faddists, minority groups, wildlife and natural land conservators, food co-ops, personal growth holistic centers, and planetary- and energy-oriented planners. By and large, these were not-for-profit collectives or networks, in some cases considered cultish or freakish, and certainly beyond the realm of my normal social circles made up of the business establishment people with whom I spent my days and nights.

The image of the establishment is an outgrowth of the historical ebb and flow of human affairs in which countercultural movements arose from time to time and, in some instances, reshaped the image of the establishment. The ancient networks of tribal and royal relationships created the aristocracy, clans, and guilds. Charismatic religious movements, the Crusades, and missionary orders challenged these closed systems. The Mafia, the revolutionary guerrillas, and the Dandy movement of the Regency milieu of Beau Brummel (1778–1840) are further countermovements wherein style and social structure were questioned in network patterns due to extreme emphasis on a particular style or belief in an entitlement.

Favoritism and monopoly can be negative attributes of networking as in the "patron clientelism" of the seventeenth-century Caracas socioeconomic system. Individuals from the elite formal networks penetrated throughout the lower classes to enable the exchange of goods, services, and support on a person-to-person basis. Patron clientelism functioned to integrate and operate a hierarchy of its own. Various types of kinship networks provided social integration of diverse types of people. The elite solidarity ties monopolized the economic, social, and political resources of the Caracas community during the seventeenth-century. The image of monopolistic networks has negatively influenced the acceptance of networking as a potential constructive process for adoption in large company management. Corporate executives are wary of network relationships which bypass the organization structure and interfere with power flow.

But to return to more modern times, during the 1960's there was a stirring of a sense of global interdependence; needs, values, and humanistic expectations became the focus of a host of informal networks where the importance of the individual was manifest. During the 1970's, and now in the 1980's, movements started in the 1960's have empowered a multitude of loosely organized networks which are becoming accepted and encouraged by enlightened leaders in the more structured parts of society. There is increasing recognition of networks as a means of transforming our institutions and of changing conduct of affairs. Networks can help organizations become more meaningful and relevant to both the personal and transcendent intersocietal global issues that beset many organizations.

NETWORKMANSHIP

It was in 1977 that I first sketched out a matrix of my own vocational, avocational, and professional activities and roles. This was a large but simple spreadsheet table of organizations and functional projects or programs with which I was involved. They were listed on the left-hand vertical column of the matrix. The horizontal top axis categorized activities, associations, and organizations into nine columns, including current employer-related directorships, professional and learned societies, educational ventures and institutions, author-lecturer positions, community, social, musical, and miscellaneous relationships. There were thirty-two identifiable roles listed at that time. Some examples were: faculty member at the Salzburg Seminars in American Studies; vice chancellor of International Academy of Management; Member of the President's Council of American Management Association, American Institute of Chemical Engineers, Institute of Directors (London), Societé de L'Ommegang (Brussels), and director of ADL–Hellas (Athens).

What I learned later was that these roles were access routes to positional networks. Membership or contributions of some sort were required in order to perform a function or assume a responsible role, i.e., belong, share, and contribute. The participation requirement had little to do with friendship or ego networking as described in Chapter 2. These thirty-two affinities or associations were either positional, attribute, or transaction-type networks. My positional role, my attribute of common concern or interest with others, or some type of dealing or exchange was involved in each of the thirty-two organizations.

When I added to this mosaic of networks my friendship or ego network contacts, a formidable multinetwork was evident. Before the advent of personal computers these contacts were maintained in four card files at the office and at home. I realized then, and even more now, that networking and networks were a way of life—and a very rewarding and personal perspective on how to get things done. Networkmanship, the art and skill of network craftmanship, imparted a quality to getting things done on a person-to-person basis which yielded mutual satisfaction and self-fulfillment.

It was not until about seven years later that I became interested in "technology transfer" of my own emerging networkmanship to making large, hierarchical organizations more effective, as distinct from the purpose of enriching my own activities. This new horizon first opened up in connection with some consulting work done overseas with boards of directors of European and Latin American corporations. The cultural barriers and "opportunity spaces" were much more apparent outside my own WASP culture. Further insights were afforded by a random series of lively seminars, colloquia, library research projects, lunchroom exchanges, and some shared client assignments with separate groups of colleagues at ADL and The Cheswick Center (Boston). These assignments were in large troubled, multinational organizations, and few stalemated, closely held companies, hung up on succession trauma, owner conflict of interests, and growing pains.

The following section unfolds some of the perspectives I came to appreciate with respect to the nature of networkmanship and its potential in organizational processes. Networkmanship promises to be flexible enough to adapt institutions to the need for new thinking about organizing and managing people in a predominantly information-based society.

NETWORKSHOP TALK

During the series of ADL after-hours networkshops mentioned on pages 108–109, we drew up a seven-point hypothesis regarding networking. We were searching for ways of identifying corporate environments which were amenable to positive networking. In addition, we were searching for a set of consulting "products" to offer the managements involved which would be useful in adapting and transforming traditional hierarchical and bureaucratic organizations to the more turbulent environment foreseen in the information society. The working hypothesis was as follows:

- A "new" paradigm is emerging in the contemporary form of social networking: personal empowerment and individual growth rather than subservience.

- The driving forces of this paradigm are changes in basic value systems. A search for the human potential, manifest by social reform and transformational movements, has created numerous activist networks. These are self-organizing, overlapping, open-ended, and fluid. They bypass hierarchy and bureaucracy and are human-centered, information-intensive, and often idealistic. They are usually disenfranchised from the "establishment."

- This decoupling process can be variously interpreted as (1) a retreat from complexity, (2) a return to tribal security, (3) a change-directed restructuring; (4) a personal search for fulfillment with more degrees of personal freedom, entrepreneurship, and creativity, or (5) management sensitivity to that which should be tolerated to promote "health" and that cannot, in any case, be literally controlled.

- Elegance in management traditionally implies symmetry, a power-driven hierarchy with control, ordered communication, and surveillance. The conventional corporate way of life is the only option offered to employees despite inevitable conflicts with personal values and goals as these change with personal experience, maturity, economic situations, and individual life interests.

- An inelegant dysfunction often results with individual and corporate career conflicts reflected in reduced organizational effectiveness at a time when external stresses, pressures, and complexities also challenge management of most institutions.

- An opportunity may be present to combine an overlay of networking concepts and practice with the hierarchical, bureaucratic paradigm of traditional organizational functioning. The purpose would be to channel and mobilize the energies of personal empowerment and individual growth in order to make them congruent with, and contributory toward, improved human resources management.

- The trick may be to manage the relationships between insensitive, power-driven, hierarchical models and individual-centered networks via a new education or learning-for-empowerment model for both individuals and organizations.

It is interesting to look back over my notes on these sessions, which ran throughout the latter part of 1983 and all of 1984. Some of the questions raised characterize the fuzzy, ambiguous, equivocal, evanescent, sub-rosa, qualitative, spontaneous, dynamic, personal, empowering, buzzwordy, confusing nature of networking. Frustrating noise levels interfere with the organizational signals indicating that networking exists or could take place—for better or for worse. Some additional considerations emerged.

Network Concepts

- Definitions of networks are far from standardized (See Appendix and Glossary for different descriptors.)

- If you tinker with a human network, will you empower or destroy it? Would not an attempt to unearth networks cause organizational reprisals?

- Networks are a normal part of human existence so the task is to learn how to develop and identify a corporate culture for positive networking. Networking will happen. How to empower it in a constructive way is the issue. It doesn't need to be invented or imposed on an organization.

- Networking can have a political relationship of facilitating countercultures, organizational transformation . . . and is a source of informal power.

- Other than a power focus, networking may be built around common concerns or interests. They may be personally or needs-driven.

- Networking is a "perpetual" process, person need-specific, not institutional in nature. The driving forces are trust, excitement, personal inquiry, and sharing.

Characteristics of Networks and Networking

- All networks are deliberate, needs-driven, and either sanctioned tacitly or tolerated in large organizations.

- The partly hidden, semiprivate nature of networks is changed when the network is exposed or formalized.

- The normal corporate culture resists networking and causes reprisals.

- Networks operate either as an underlay or overlay to hierarchy and bureaucracy.

- Environmental nourishment of networks might help resolve ethical issues, privacy concerns, and implications of manipulation or other possible negative impacts on organizational effectiveness.

- Power or influence may accumulate for networkers who share a common position or ideology. As such, networks may be a precursor to institutionalization.

- Social network ties are beyond the capability of any network analysis techniques. Block model analysis of large networks, as developed at Yale University, have been applied to nineteen networks (in 1982) to develop a taxonomy of block commonalities which is useful in comparative analysis of organizations. These varied as a function of characteristics of the block in some cases, and in others as a function of the characteristics of the entire organization. Boundary permeability and causation issues were found to be important, as well as size and environment of the organization.

Possible Uses of Networks

- Remedying particular organizational problems (lack of innovativeness, bureaucratic barriers, pockets of employee discontent and misunderstandings, political cliques) or improving the interfacing between organizations and units within organizations or between different classes of institutions (town-gown understandings, political-business supportive relationships, law enforcement agencies and the public).

- Changing public, membership, or employee opinions to a different value system, or social or political orientation: lobbying, consciousness-raising on global problems (acid rain, third-world connections, alternative power sources, protection of endangered species).

- Building interinstitutional coalitions: establishing joint cooperation between hospitals and clinics, universities and communities, or competing religious institutions.

- Achieving organizational change: moving a company culture from an existing state to a target model state of cultural change.

- Strengthening and empowering professional societies through peer communications, scheduled events and meetings, publications, and the building of status roles through a hierarchy of titles and honors.

- Providing a consulting and counselling resource through a network of knowledgeable and influential contacts (A celebrity-type example of this is New York–based Kissinger Associates, Inc. Some twenty-eight U.S. and foreign multinational corporations and banks pony up $150,000 to $250,000 annually as a retainer to obtain the advice of Dr. Kissinger and his vast network of contacts. His lifelong association with the Rockefellers, Harvard, and international connections form a power grid of global proportions at the "celestial level" according to *Business Week* (December 2, 1985). Kissinger Associates provides introductions, geopolitical advice, access to power brokerage, international representation, prestige and consulting through the blending of public and private networks of Kissinger Associates.)

So I come back to my theme: Do I Network? You Can Bet Your Life I Do. Networking has been good to me. I believe it has done some good for others. I've learned that networks die easily. The decay rate is more rapid than the build-up rate. Networkmanship is a skill to be learned by experimentation, and it's fun and rewarding. It's not the organization chart, it's the people.

Chapter 11

How to Design and Set Up a Network

> Networkers are already motivated or
> they wouldn't be in the network . . .
> the biggest problem networks have is
> how to pay the phone bill.
> —*Byron Kennard*[1]

Networks are essentially free-form and self-organizing. Hazel Henderson, author of *Creating Alternative Futures*, describes a network as a combination of an invisible college and a modern version of the Committee of Correspondence, which our revolutionary forefathers used as vehicles for political change.[2]

A consistent theme found in most networking is the search for alternative solutions which conventional wisdom may not suggest. Networks offer cooperation rather than competition. The fact that networks are decentralized in concept makes the search for solutions easier to understand, broader in scope and reach. Decentralization benefits can be ideally maximized by networking. A key is the possible restoring of accountable flesh, as individuals take action within a social system. With such personal accountability comes personal dignity, motivation, and reward.

Designing and setting up a network can serve a variety of purposes. Usually networks are established for the purpose of finding alternative pathways for personal or group action. Networks may be for (1) enhancing our intellectual, social, and leisure activities, (2) keeping in touch with certain people who share common interests or concerns, (3) exploring the value and potential of a more formally organized endeavor, (4) keeping informed and trading information with others, (5) influencing, politically or otherwise, and learning from others who elect to network with you, (6) linking individuals with individuals, organizations with organizations, or individuals with organizations, (7) affecting change in complex organizations or situations by offering alternative methods of increasing awareness, unfreezing attitudes, and refreezing them in changed directions, and finally, (8) expanding, without undue risk but with lower acquisition costs and improved stability, awareness of what we personally have to offer others. Given one or more purposes it is easy to design and create a network.[3]

Anthropologists and sociologists have used the concept of networking as a metaphor for over one hundred years. Virginia H. Hine and Luther P. Gerlach, anthropologists, gave us the first theoretical framework for setting up networks as "an adaptive pattern of social organization for the global society of the future."[4] They conceived this pattern based on their fieldwork with two subcultures: the Pentecostal movement and the Black Power movement.

The basic paradigm has been described in lay terms in Virginia Hine's classic essay.[5] The concept goes under the acronym SP(I)N, pronounced "spin." It stands for an anthropological mouthful: segmented, polycephalous (ideological) network. Autonomous segments that are organizationally self-sufficient can stand alone and survive the elimination of all the others that comprise the first element of the equation. The word *polycephalous* means "many-headed" and in a human network there are many leaders for many tasks or points of view . . . networks have multiple pools of responsibility, awareness, and information. Hine wrote, "But the power of the unifying idea adds a qualitatively different element to the equation." The I of the SP(I)N gives the concept of its symbolic power . . . the deep personal commitment networkers have to a few basic tenets shared by all.

In early 1981, I created a temporary network of my own for the purpose of assessing, for a client, certain technology trends around the globe. The trends pertained to advanced composite compositions of matter, new polymeric materials, and the future impact of certain new, world-class petrochemical sources of supply springing up in the Middle East. Initially this was both an ego and a positional network. The contacts made in Europe, Africa, the Middle East, Latin America, Canada, and the Pacific Basin were all personal friends. The contact was made either by correspondence, or, in some cases, by a personal visit. Later on the network included friends of friends who were respected in the fields of interest.

The objective was to get a periodic panel view of technical, economic, and social forces at work, along with possible interventions by governments, and to track the intercourse between private industry and public sector producers and consumers. After initial exchanges by letter, the network participant role was telescoped down to only four internationally experienced and technically qualified individuals.

We organized an advisory council and arranged quarterly meetings to serve the client with a running, interpretive evaluation of what was going on in the world in the areas with which he was concerned. The institutionalization and shake-out of the original network did not destroy the vital nature of the input and exchange. The meetings and the sharing and testing of views were kept to a loosely organized system of face-to-face, telephone, and written exchanges. In this example, the design and creation of an initial network led to a small, functional organization. The sequel to the network was a formal advisory group. It acted as a sounding board and an early warning, look-out group, created after the network experiment warranted some formalization of process and a clarified charter.

NETWORK START-UPS

A logical approach to designing your network can consist of the following eight steps:

Step One: Purpose and Objectives

Clarify the purpose(s) of the proposed network. This may be any of the eight notional purposes listed previously in this chapter or others that suit your fancy.

Step Two: Resource Inventory

Inventory your personal "ego network" and your "positional network." Define yourself as a resource. This is the simple task of, as objectively as possible, taking stock of your personal and material resources, such as, your knowledge, skills, experiences, contacts, intuitive and instinctive interests, values, beliefs, articles of faith, aspirations, expectations, and natural talents. In addition, your material assets may be useful to others in the proposed network. Material assets can include office equipment, communications facilities, club memberships, office facilities, business and personal card files, transportation, etc.

Your occupational or professional position affords certain resources including access to individuals in specialized or status roles. Memberships in learned societies, professional organizations, and fraternal and social orders all provide "positional network" resources for building a new independent network.

Step Three: Resource Gap

Estimate or identify resources which you find missing in Step Two and which are needed to accomplish the purpose(s) of your network. These become target resources, i.e., network nodes or linkages to be built or explored as your network swings into action. Searching for such resources can be done through your own "ego" or "positional" network contacts, by a survey of literature and activities underway in the field of interest, or by field interviews on the issue or topic to be addressed.

Step Four: Structural Nature

Decide on the kind of network which intuitively seems most appropriate to serve the purpose(s). At least two kinds of networks can be distinguished from the start: attribute networks and transactional networks. In an attribute network, persons are connected when they share some commonality, such as, similarity of views, life goals, sex, nationality, race, education, or status. Transactional networks are different in that they focus on the exchanges that occur among a group of individuals.

Incidentally, these two networks define two initial network strategies. As outlined by Dr. Fombrun, University of Pennsylvania, when starting with an attribute network, exchanges are seen as dependent characteristics or consequences of the network pattern. If we begin with a transactional network, individual attributes become the causes of the transactional configuration.[6]

Step Five: Actor Assessment

Assess the proposed networkers as to their probable role in the communications function of the network. This means identifying those individuals whom you perceive as having a great deal of influence on others (not dominance) and who are the focus of most communications within the group of persons in Step Three that you hope to reach. These can be "stars" in your network and nodes in the structure.

Peg the individuals in your own ego and positional networks that you expect will be less communicative. These are the "isolates." Identify individuals in your own existing networks who serve as intermediates within some other set of persons. These are the "liaisons" or "linkers." They serve as connections between the nodes. Other linkages may be physical information sources, rather than human, i.e., a computer data base, a library, a newsletter, or a book. Identify the boundary spanning individuals known as "gatekeepers" who can serve as important linking mechanisms (or barriers) between organizations and the environment external to the boundary or domain in which they operate. For example, in large companies certain individuals in, say, an R&D department may control exchange with other departments or projects only on those tasks which are locally oriented.

Step Five is when you begin to use the structure of your network. The first inquiries and sharing of information will be with the stars, weavers, linkers, and selected isolates.

Step Six: Networking Process

Consider the process of networking to be used. If your primary experience has been limited to highly structured organizations, such as, a large business corporation, government, or religious hierarchy, you will find networking processes differ considerably and can be much more fun. As Tim Heald puts it, "Networking, like sex, is one of the few activities at which a gifted and enthusiastic amateur has built-in advantage over the purely professional."[7]

The process which you may find most effective in your own networking is one that encourages relationships with those with whom you have or can establish a collegial connection. Conversely, you skip or discourage connections where one person is dominant and nonegalitarian. Ideally, there is no dominate-subordinate equation in a network. The relationship or connection made in a network is a thing in itself separate from either participant. If you don't want or can't establish a relationship separate from the actors involved, your network process may become influenced by the control of the relationship and run the risk of introducing a personal bias of those serving as stars, weavers, linkers, gatekeepers, or isolates.

The connection which has a life of its own is one of trust. Trust develops over a period of time where exchanges take place. Competition has no role in network relationships, contrary to the essential nature of dominant-subordinate relationships in hierarchical structures. The collegial nature of the networking process works on the freedom to explore associations and information exchange.

Dr. Allen Parker, founder and executive director of the Center on Technology and Society, Cambridge, Massachusetts, and Dr. Marianne Hedin, research associate at the Center, studied sixty innovation networks in the field of education to seek patterns of change involved in the networking processes. They found that management by objectives does not work well in networking. Rather, they specify five "positions" which take place sequentially, with some bypassing and recycling as innovative ideas or problems to be solved move from their origin to fruition or solution.[8]

Briefly, Position I is where isolated innovators and problem solvers become willing to share the idea or problem with others. Position II is called an unintentional informal network of dispersed people who know others and make contacts on a nonprearranged basis. If this exchange and interaction creates a strong common concern, the process moves to Position III, intentional informal network. Meetings, newsletters, and more formal communications begin. Funds are sought, if needed. If this step proceeds, Position IV, the formal network, is reached. The Position IV effort establishes identity and purpose, participants are listed, meetings or exchanges are planned. At this point the network may have achieved its goal and is often disbanded.

Alternately, Position V may be sought and reached. This is the institutionalized network creature. Centralization takes place with a facilitating center in a nonprofit corporation, or a wing of an established institution. Funding, formal organization, and structure are introduced. If everyone is not careful a bureaucracy will grow and destroy the nature of the network by introducing competition and hierarchy. If a competitive culture develops the comparative analysis with others may limit the freedom of participants, elitism creeps in, and the withholding of network information gathered from others becomes a practice to preserve the institution. Position V, when routinized, can be shifted to established professional societies, associations, or consortium of organizations. The human network features then have to exist in conflict with institutionalized goals and norms. The essence of collegial networking may be jeopardized.

Step Seven: Informational Data Base

Start a repository for your information and ideas. There may be more than one data base. This can be a computer log, a library, a card file, or any other means that is comfortable and accessible for you to use as you nurture and empower your network.

One network created in 1984 was facilitated by a telemailbox at The Cheswick Center. Key associates in various locations are linked by TELEnet and GOVERNnet, a newly created computer network service, through their "electronic mailbox" personal computers. Messaging goes on at all hours in a biocoastal mode, at any place, without face-to-face meetings, which are difficult to achieve due to the other full-time pursuits of the principals involved. The individuals check their electronic mailboxes, when convenient, for the stored messages. Upon command, these are displayed on the screens of their portable, four-pound, personal computers.

Step Eight: Action

Remember that the core of the network concept is to exchange information, expedite the process, recognize patterns of information processing, and learn. To get going, make a trial run as an initial stage. The following are some of the considerations on where and how to start.

1. The skills of networking require the ability to combine appreciation of problem structure, "opportunity space," human behavior, and symbolism. Appreciation of these four items must be accompanied by some knowledge of where the interested parties may be, e.g., industry sectors, educational domains, government information sources, communities, organizations, and friends operating in the field of interest or exploration.

2. Recognize that when a little help from your friends—your ego network—becomes an outright imposition it's time to observe some networking protocol and a few courtesies, such as timing your requests, watching for expenses incurred, avoiding excessive requests, respecting your contact's sense of timing, being specific about the inquiry, being appreciative, and providing feedback. Don't abuse your network. Some of the most common abuses are in job-hunting situations, the ensnaring of friends for charity advisory roles, and in seeking information for investment purposes.

3. Obey the conventional, common sense "rules" of the networking process. Patricia Wagner and Leif Smith have published a popularized pamphlet guide as a tool for introducing persons to networking. Their four rules are useful: "Don't be boring, listen, ask questions, and don't make assumptions." The "networking game" is an easy way to "the art of discovering patterns in the world and making useful connections for ourselves and for others. It is about weaving new options into our safety nets."9

4. Keep three indices in mind to track the effectiveness of your networking. Sociologists have worked this system out for measuring interchange of information in a network. *Centrality* is the tendency of one person, or of a unit's members, to be cited (referred to in the networking process) by others in the network, or by others outside the unit. *Integration* is the tendency of a networker to cite other networkers. *Dependence* is the tendency of an individual networker, or a member of some unit, to cite networkers or others outside the unit or network. By keeping tabs on these three indices you can get some measure of the effectiveness and activity of your network *if*, for some reason, you have need to assess the vitality and effectiveness of the network.

5. Start-ups should have a focus rather than a specific goal. If we knew specific goals it wouldn't be networking. For example, if the purpose of the network is to raise consciousness about the protection of quality of an inland lake, articulate that general focus in clear terms, not specific goals. Specific goals can come later and their pursuit handled by processes other than networking, i.e., task forces, projects, or organizational programs.

6. Have a "mother" or "father" figure, a leader who is the initiator, arranger, and central communicator, and one who needs or knows what's up and keeps track. This can be an executive secretary, a staff expert on a paid or volunteer basis.

7. Create a modest, regular "poop sheet" or newsletter as a regular communications vehicle. Use computers if the network "messages" by electronic means, or the mail. The newsletter should be quick to produce and easy to read—not a professional reference or research journal. Don't make a chore out of it.

8. Publish a list of members. *Connections*, the Bulletin of the International Network for Social Network Analysis, Toronto, Canada, publishes a directory of all INSNA members grouped by disciplines and interest areas, with a sentence or two about what each member is up to. The Human Systems Management (HSM) Circle, Fordham University, New York, publishes a list of all Circle members and their affiliations. Anyone interested in networking with another can go directly to him or her.

9. Identify a group you know for initial contact, rather than a committee of networkers, to start your inquiry and information exchange. Don't institutionalize or structure the networking. It's not the organization structure or network chart that counts. It's the people.

10. Set some target event to exchange fruits of the networking. If the project warrants feedback to the contributors, set a tentative target date to share your findings, thinking, solution, or perplexity. Those who volunteer to network with you will probably want some feedback.

As indicated in the chapter introduction, networkers are already motivated or they wouldn't be in the network. This will be true of your personal "ego" and "positional" networkers. Operating a network is a subtle behavioral process of creating information exchange and of learning. Properly empowered through networking, "our self interests can be transformed into a personally and intellectually satisfying mutuality," according to Yale University professor of psychology, Dr. Seymour B. Sarason.

Appendix

Networkspeak

> Rhinestone vocabulary: Originally, fashion terminology for high style terms used to describe the latest vogue in such "gems" as: hot pants, civilized clothes, ethnic, savage, mini-midi-maxi, etc. Used in reference to stylish words of the day; used particularly in promotional lingo, such as in the marketing and advertising leagues.[1]

New words, needed but often confusing, are born daily. Such buzzwords, verbojuice, and zipvocab are useful. But, you need a guide and glossary to understand them. Modern networks are no exception.

To begin with, let's look at how the concept of networking was expressed in the myths and metaphors of various ancient cultures.

SOME CULTURAL DEFINITIONS OF NETWORKS

To the Chinese the stars of the firmament were a "net of heaven."

Christians spoke about the unbreakable net of the Church and the ensnaring net of the devil. The disciples were referred to as the "fishers of man."

To Egyptians "the net of the underworld" was a common phrase for the human network of thieves and outcasts.

Greco-Romans perceived Hephaestos/Vulcan as "smith gods" and "gods who bind," thereby establishing a celestial set of connections between gods.

To a Scandinavian, a network was an attribute of the goddess Ran, the "ravisher," a different connotation of networking.

In the Orphic Fish Cult, like the Semitic, the word of divinity was "the great net encircling heaven and earth," in essence, a communications network.

The Sumero-Semitic fish cult believed "the great net encircles heaven and earth;" it was an emblem of gods who bind. Bel was invoked as the "catching net" and Marduk overcame Tiamat with a net; Ishtar was a goddess of the net. In Babylon, the rope or bond represented the cosmic principle uniting all things, and the law which supports and holds all things together.

A Taoist refers to heaven's net or a net of unity where there is a common concern. In Temuz mythology there was "Lord of snares." Marduk, a master binder, functioned with noose, snares, and nets; Shamash was armed with snares and cord; Enil and his wife, Nkhursag, were lunar divinities who caught the guilty with nets; and Ninurta was lord of the encompassing net.

In Teutonic lands, there was a ceremony to celebrate the binding of kings.

Anthropologists and sociologists have used network imagery for over a century as a metaphor for their research into insights of human communication and behavior. More recent scholars have introduced certain new and coined words to convey contemporary concepts of human networks and social networking. With due apology to these anthropologists, some of this modern network vocabulary—networkspeak to reflect the idiom—can be used either for intellectual one-upmanship or, better, as a real help in communicating a specialized meaning.

I refer to buzzwords, generally, and the corresponding networkspeak, as those words or phrases used by, say, a networking ingroup for rapid communication within their network. There is limited regard for whether or not the meaning is understood outside the network group. Networkspeak refers also to the verbal, intellectual one-upmanship of the slang, jargon, and pseudo-tribal language used by relatively small groups for their own benefit and to help isolate the networkers from hoi polloi. Networkspeak is sort of a pro's prose.

Webster's unabridged *New International Dictionary*, second edition, contains some 550,000 vocabulary entries considered useful for those employing the English language. It is estimated that there are over one million English words available, if you wish to dig them out of other sources. The average educated person is said to understand only about 60,000 and probably uses around 30,000 words. This means that with the exception of some philologists, lexicographers, and linguists, substantially less than 10 percent of the words currently available in our English language are known to well-educated people.

This limited utilization of available words apparently is true for other civilized languages, according to Columbia University professor Mario Andrew Pei. The basic reason for this is partly attributable to the fact that the various branches of human activity develop specialized vocabularies.

As these particular disciplines and endeavors grow and mature, so do the vocabularies concerned with them. Each field finds it necessary to create new words, borrow ones from other or older fields, adapt, combine, and create a vocabulary of its own, such as the vocabulary of the chemists which is derived originally from the alchemists, physicians, and lawyers, plus other professions and areas of intellectual activity. Modern networkers are not alone in this tendency toward networkspeak.

When a buzzword achieves a valuable role in communication, it becomes a part of more widely used language and may even cease to be set aside as something special. The computer world continues to add computerese in which new words run in packs. After a while they become part of many people's everyday vocabulary. Some examples are, *programming, software, command menu, data base, module, electronic memory, electronic spreadsheet.*

And so it is with networkspeak, the "High Talk" of networkers. Intellectual High Talk and ordinary Low Talk are alike in intent. Each is designed to be a private language understandable to members of an ingroup but causing perplexity to outsiders. Both disregard normal words and phrases.

"Low Talk" originates in closely related groups, particularly among the economically and culturally disadvantaged. Because their lives are centered on actions rather than words, they acquire a limited, vivid vocabulary and use a grammar of their own with a minimum of syntax and little punctuation.

On the other hand, "High Talk" comes from those who prefer to speak in multisyllable words, such as *ideation*, *optimization*, *probabilistic transitions*, *lemma*, *structurally equivalent nodes*, *self-balancing networks*, and *class structure*. The danger of some High Talk is its cloak of respectability even when the meaning and intended use are not sound, or when the High Talk is used primarily to impress peers, obscure, or merely to be affected.

With the current interest in social or human networking we need a glossary to help us pick our way through the webs of networkers' noise and activities. The "rhinestone virtues" of some of the terms now in vogue may eventually fade away. Or, the words will grow in legitimate use for those who explore the exciting concepts of human networking and social networks in our larger organizations.

The following glossary is a sampling of the buzzwords currently abounding in the field of social and human networking. By no means a complete listing, the collection waffles over a bit into electronic communications, as the integration of human networking with computers is part of the social network movement.

On pages 148–151 of the Notes section are sources where these terms have been defined by one or another author, not necessarily an original citation. Rather, the cited text can be referenced to provide a broader context in which to understand the use of networkspeak.

GLOSSARY

Amiability Tilt This is the notion that the major activity of social networks is to ferry support (i.e., contact) between particular members. However, the amiability tilt overlooks the third dimension of social networks, namely, conflict. Overlapping between conflict, support, and contact exists in models of social networking and networks.

Attribute Networks These are networks linking individuals who share a commonality, such as, similarity of attributes, goals, sex, status.

Barter Networks Exchange of skills, services, and products occurs among many client groups. They are often nonprofit networks which offer free or minimal cost services to all target group clients. Low-income and younger members of the community often participate and benefit from these barter networks. Other barter organizations are on a profit basis where participants pay tax on goods or services exchanged through them.[1]

Booster Network This is an artifically created or ersatz network designed primarily for advancement of members (despite frequent protests to the contrary). The term was first coined by Sinclair Lewis (1885–1951).

Boundary Spanner An individual who links one organization with another.

Centrality The term refers to the degree to which relations are guided by the formal hierarchy.[2]

Clustering This is a structural characteristic of a network; it refers to the number of dense regions in the network.[3]

Coalitions   These are perceived linkages among several individuals who believe that their ability to dominate organizational relationships is greater as a group than as individuals. Coalitions can also be used as individual descriptors when the analysis focuses on a person's membership or non-membership in specific emergent groups.[4]

Collateral Organization   This organization type is similar to the matrix or grid structure, multidimensional structure, or global matrix program management and project management architecture. It is also termed the two-boss model for some people who report simultaneously to two superiors, one in the functional design and one in the matrix or business team respect. It consists of a web or network of fresh problem-solving linkages, mainly vertical, that slice through the formal structure. A matrix is horizontally integrated while a collateral organization is linked both vertically and horizontally.[5]

Computer-Conferencing Network   This is a system for linking people together, using personal computers, communication technology and conference software. Office or home terminals are connected through telephone lines to communications satellites which in turn are linked to a central computer. Messages are transmitted at the individual's convenience via the computer to the terminals of other participants. These messages are displayed on video screens and may be reproduced in hard copy on a printer.

Connectedness   This is the extent to which group members identify with the goals of other members of their groups. It is a measure of group cohesiveness.[6]

Cooptive Corporate Actor Network   The total set of establishments represented on a firm's board of directors by ownership, direct interlocking, or direct interlocking through financial institutions.[7]

Cosmopolite   A communications network term referring to an individual who has a relatively high degree of communication within the system's environment.[8]

Density   The number of actual links in a network as a ratio of the number of possible links (see *Connectedness*).

Dispersed Networks   Our mobile societies, global professions, multinational institutions make our social world more interactive, more interdependent, and intercommunicative. As a result networks which were once of the highly connected type become dispersed. Networks form only with some and not all the component individuals because of the broad scope and lack of common external boundary.

Diwanniya   An Arabic term for informal networking encounters. *Diwanniyas* are unofficial meetings with a serious purpose in addition to conviviality. The meetings are usually hosted by one person as a gathering of equals for discussion and exchange of views rather than a patronage of the host. It is not appropriate to make definite commitments or settlements (as is done in clinching a business deal), but the key issues can be talked about in detail anyway. The network sessions are often a preliminary to official discussions which take place among the principals at a later stage. *Diwanniyas* differ from *majlis*, the formal, official meetings during working hours on a patron–client basis. A *bashka* is a close network of friends who meet regularly for convivial company, dining, cards, and socializing.

Ego-Network   The network for which an actor is the "ego" consists of all persons with whom the actor has a direct relationship and the relationships among those persons.[10] Such network models are also described as primary stars, primary zones, first-order zones, or personal networks. They can be anchored on any aggregation of persons as, for example, families, or corporations.

Federation   This is a linkage network which is distinguished from others in that a federation has the control and management of the activities of the network. In most types of linkage networks, the organization involved retains control over its own interorganizational activities, especially when there are few organizations in the network.[11] One organization may be more able to influence the direction of the network than another, especially if relative dependencies among the linked organizations are not equal. But control of their joint activities will rest with the organizations themselves. In a federation, however, affiliated organizations agree to relinquish control over certain activities to the federation's management. In return, affiliated organizations expect the federation's management to minimize the complexity of the linkage network and reduce environmental uncertainty.

Fly-Eyed   These networks tolerate, and even encourage, many perspectives about goals and means. Although it may appear the network sees only one point of view, on closer inspection, the network has one apparent eye that embodies a plethora of others. Like its transparent, two-winged, flying relative, the network is *fly-eyed*.[12]

Gatekeeper   A member of a communications network who prevents information overload by filtering and screening messages; a star who also links the social unit with external domains.[13]

Groupies   Those who have an unthinking association with a group, like the members of a gang. They need most of all to feel safety and belonging, so they pay attention to the commonalities among people in minimized differences. Groupies can be emotionally swayed by charismatic leaders and peer pressure, but they are learning important lessons; to establish rapport and comply with group demands.[14] (see *Hologroupists*)

Guanxi   The Chinese term for the complex sociological network of personal relationships that still grease the working of that society.

Hierarchy   Any established order based on value, status, priority, importance, rank, relativity, personal taste, and/or natural law. Hierarchies
can be distinctly subjective (my dog is better than your dog), or universally constant (on a ship the captain gives the orders). Hierarchies provide a system of incentives while establishing boundaries. We make the
grade, move on to the next level, or claw our way up. The physical mani-
festation of a hierarchy is a pyramid with a supreme ruler at the top and
the subordinates and descending classifications below.[15]

The word *hierarchy* comes from the Greek root *hieros* or "sacred"
and *archos* meaning "leader." *Hieraechies* is Greek for "high priest."[16]
In application to the architecture of complex systems, hierarchy simply
means a set of Chinese boxes of a particular kind, "the recursion continuing as long as the patience of the craftsman holds out."

A hierarchy mirrors natural law. Corporate hierarchies are not unlike a hive of honeybees or an ant colony. Priorities shift and change as
our lives become an intricate series of overlapping pyramids. We talk
about chains of command, totem poles, ladders of success, class distinc-
tions, and pecking orders (which are all based on barnyard reality). Social hierarchies have been with us since the dawn of time. "Caste" systems are still very much a part of life in India, Asia, Africa, and
Nantucket.

Highly Connected Networks   Family networks are of this type with the
common blood or marriage ties, a kinship, and system of close affective
(emotional) and ascriptive (attributal) realtionships in an otherwise predominantly competitive society. Rural area farmers, faculty members in
a remote school, coal miners, and artist colonies are also examples
where networks are highly connected.

Hologroupists   Persons embracing a whole undertaking or group. Whereas
teams divide up the task and synergists cooperate for efficiency, hologroupists go a step further. They become the context for the task. Hologroupists also understand the other relationship abilities and use them
naturally when appropriate and don't depend on a single style. They act
with an awareness of the whole with a sense that separateness is a state
of mind. They see through outer differences to a conscious oneness with
the total environment.[17]

Horizontal Differentiation   The degree to which different job areas are
represented in a given network.[18]

Hydra-Headed   Describing a network that speaks with many equivalent
but different voices at the same time. Whereas hierarchies were originally constructed with steps up a pyramid of ranks to a pinnacle that
housed and exalted one revered leader or board of directors, networks
have many leaders and few, if any, rungs of power. They are like the Hy-
dra, the nine-headed serpent which grew two heads each time one was
cut off by Hercules.[19]

Integration The tendency of the unit's members to cite one another.[20]

Isolates Individuals who are seen as involved in almost no communication within the group; they are decoupled from the network.[21]

Kinterlock A concept introduced to describe the connections created when a director of one company is related through kinship to the director of another company. (British origin).

Levels Like hierarchies in all systems, networks have many levels of organizations. Unlike hierarchies in which lower-level people, such as secretaries, have considerably less importance and power than those above, networks function with the recognition of the integration of importance of all levels.[22]

Liaisons Individuals who serve as intermediaries among various emergent work groups within a department; individuals in a network who are not members of a cluster but who link two or more clusters.[23]

Linkage Intensity Strength of the relationship between individuals in a network.[24]

Linkage Reciprocity The degree to which a relation is commonly perceived and agreed on by all parties involved, i.e., the degree of symmetry.[25]

Massingberd 500, The Five hundred key network families in Great Britain who have consistently produced "men and women of prominence" over at least three generations. They were first classified by genealogist Hugh Montgomery-Massingberd.[26]

Metanetworks Networks that exist to network other networks. Examples: The Networking Institute (West Newton, Massachusetts); The Metasystems Design Group (Arlington, Virginia); Microcomputer Information Support Tools (MIST) (Lake Oswego, Oregon).

Multiplexity In a network, the degree to which pairs of individuals are linked by multiple relations.[27]

Negative Network A situation in which network membership is a liablity rather than an advantage, and a member is discriminated against; rather like inverted snobbery.[28]

Network A network is a web of free-standing participants linked by one or more shared values. Networks are composed of self-reliant people and of independent works.[29] The term "network" is the communications analogue to the sociological concept of group; but "network" is distinct from "group" in that it refers to a number of individuals (or other units) who persistently interact with one another in accordance with established patterns. Networks can be measured sociometrically, but they are otherwise not visually obvious.

Network Bridge An individual who is a member of multiple clusters in the network (linking).[30]

Network Clique A set of actors in a network who are connected to one another by strong relations. Examples are: families, playgroups, com-

munities, primary groups characterized by intimate face-to-face association and cooperation. Friendship networks are cliques. The more
cohesive the group, the more friendship ties there are within the group,
and the more active the process of communication which goes on within
the group, and the greater the effect of the process of communication in
producing uniformity of attitudes, opinions, and behavior.[31]

Network Openness   Number of actual external links of a social unit as a ratio of the number of possible external links.[32]

Network Stability   The degree to which a network pattern changes over
time.[33]

Organization   Identical social entities pursuing multiple objectives through
the coordinated activities and relations among members and objects.
Such a social system is open-ended and dependent for survival on other
individuals and subsystems in the larger entity-society.[34]

Structures of mutual expectations attached to roles which define
what each of its members shall expect from others and from himself.

A conjunction of procedures, interpretations, behaviors, and puz-
zles.

Organizing   A consensually validated grammar for reducing equivocality
by means of sensible, interlocked behaviors.[35]

People Networks   A multileadered netting of sovereign participants
threaded by common ideology; decentralized, segmentary, and reticu-
late.[36]

Positional Networks   Contacts stemming from one's structural, occupational positions in one or more network or hierarchical systems. The
term also applies to role connections in a social or professional set, club,
or association.

Reachability   The average number of links between any two individuals in
the network.[39]

Reciprocity   The degree to which there is two-way communication in a
work group.[37]

Reticulist   One who has networking skills. The skills of network management require the ability to combine an appreciation of problem structure and "opportunity space" with an appreciation of political structure.[38]

Separatives   Those who prefer to work on their own. When people begin to
break free of imposed rules and values, they may seek a mentor or
guidelines until they learn to trust themselves more fully. Others may go
to extremes, rejecting all rules.[40]

Social Networks   A specific set of linkages among a defined group of persons with the additional property that the characteristics of these linkages as a whole may be used to interpret the social behavior of the persons involved.

Societal Network   A definite, directed graph in which individuals are represented by nodes and relations between individuals by labeled arcs. Each individual undergoes transitions at discrete instances of time so that the societal network may be thought of as a deterministic, dynamic process.[42]

Sociogram   A graphic representation of relationships among individuals in a hierarchy network, or other organization. A set of elements related to one another through multiple interconnections, i.e., a network.[43]

SP(I)N   Pronounced "spin," this is an easy acronym which stands for "segmented polycephalous (ideological) network. It refers to an adaptive pattern of social organization for the global society of the future.[44] Contrasted with a bureaucracy that collapses like a table when a leg is cut off, SP(I)N is composed of autonomous segments, any of which could survive the elimination of all the others. A segment stands alone and with other segments. In networks, anthropologists observe that there are leaders for different tasks.

Star(s)   Individuals who are seen as having a great deal of influence on the jobs of most group members and who are the focus of most communications within the group.[45] Also, the individual in a network with the highest number of nominations.[46]

Super–Subs   Either superordinates (bosses) or subordinates (underlings) who are afraid of losing group protection. Super-subs try to impose order on the universe through doctrines and procedures. They need to know precisely what the world expects of them. And through precise definitions of roles, they learn to be good leaders and good followers.[47]

Symbiotics   Those who form loose associations. After gaining some measure of independence, they may next seek to associate with others of like mind to form teams of loose confederations with particular interests. Team members share abilities, learn to negotiate, and compromise. They create natural hierarchies based on competence and delegate responsibility to those with expertise.[48]

Synergists   Those who believe the whole is more than the sum of of its parts.[49]

Transactional Content   Involves four types of exchange and is a property of a network expression of effect, influence attempt, exchange of information, and exchange of goods or services.[50]

Transactional Networks   Those which focus on the exchanges that occur among a set of individuals.

Vertical Differentiation   The degree to which different organizational hierarchy levels are represented in a given network.[51]

Wholeparts   Networks are composed of self-reliant and autonomous participants; people in organizations who simultaneously function as "independent wholes" and as "interdependent parts." Wholeparts is a fundamental feature of networks.[52]

NOTES

CHAPTER 1

1. Seymour B. Sarason, "Redefining Self As A Resource," J. C. Penney *Forum*, March 1983, pp. 12–13.

2. W. Alec Jordan, "Of Nymphs, GWRK's and Other Amazing Stories," *Chemical Technology*. Vol. 6, November 1976, pp. 672–675.

CHAPTER 2

1. J. C. Cooper, *An Illustrated Encyclopedia of Traditional Symbols*, Thames and Hudson, London, 1978, p. 111.

2. K. S. Weick, "Educational Organizations as Loosely Coupled Systems," *Administrative Science Quarterly*, No. 21, 1976, pp. 1–19.

3. Jessica Lipnack and Jeffrey Stamps, *Networking: The First Report and Directory*, Doubleday, New York, 1982.

4. Everett M. Rogers and Judith K. Larsen, *Silicon Valley Fever: The Growth of High Technology Culture*, Basic Books, New York, 1984.

5. In the 1930's, Jacob Moreno invented "sociometry" as a method of collecting material on who relates to whom and of graphically displaying the

relationships. His method was originally used in a reform school as a way of grouping together, in the same cottage, girls who could get along with one another and of finding natural leaders to keep the peace.

6. A. Bavelas, "An Experimental Approach to Organizational Communication," *Personnel*, 1951, pp. 27, 366–371.

7. H. J. Leavitt, "Some Effects of Certain Communication Patterns on Group Performance," *Journal of Abnormal and Social Psychology*, No. 46, 1951, pp. 38–50.

8. Marilyn Ferguson, *The Aquarian Conspiracy: Personal and Social Transformation in the 1980's*, J. P. Tarcher, Los Angeles, 1980.

9. Hazel Henderson, *Creating Alternative Futures: The End of Economies*, Berkley Publishing, New York, 1978.

10. Virginia H. Hine, "The Basic Paradigm of a Future Socio-Cultural System," *World Issues*, April/May 1977; also coauthor with Luther Gerlach of *People, Power, Change*, Bobbs-Merrill, New York, 1970; and of *Lifeway Leap: The Dynamics of Change in America*, University of Minnesota Press, Minneapolis, 1972.

11. Lipnack and Stamps, *Networking*, p. 1.

12. Ibid.

13. Ibid., pp. 222–234.

14. For those interested in more history about social network studies abroad, the following references are typical of the host of such papers tapped to illustrate examples in this chapter.

David H. Bayley, "Learning About Crime—The Japanese Experience," *Public Interest*, 1976, pp. 55–68.

George A. Collier, "The Determinants Of Highland Maya Kinship," *Journal of Family History*, Vol. 3, No. 4, 1978, pp. 439–453.

Ned Levine, "Old Culture—New Culture: A Study Of Migrants In Ankara, Turkey," *Social Forces*, Vol. 51, No. 3, 1973, pp. 355–368.

V. I. Liakh, "The Communist Party's Guidance Of The Komsomol During Socialist Construction 1921-37," *Ukraine Kyi Istorychnyi Zhurnal* (USSR), No. 1, pp. 61–66.

Ayse Oncu, "Inter-Organizational Networks And Social Structure: Turkish Chambers Of Industry," *Journal of International Social Science* (France), Vol 3, No. 4, 1979, pp. 646–660.

B. Marie Perinbam, "Social Relations In The Trans-Saharan And Western Sudanese Trade: An Overview," *Comparative Studies in Society and History* (Great Britain), Vol. 15, No. 4, 1973, pp. 416–436.

Marc Howard Ross, "Two Styles Of Political Participation In An African City," *American Journal of Political Science*, Vol. 17, No. 1, 1973, pp. 1–22.

CHAPTER 3

1. C. F. von Weizsäcker, ed., *Evolution and Entropy Increase, Open Systems I*, Klett, Stuttgart, 1974.

2. Jean Piaget, *Structuralism*, Basic Books, New York, 1970.

3. P. Watzlawick, *How Real is Real?*, Vintage Books, New York, 1976, pp. 24–25.

4. Ronald S. Burt, *Toward a Structural Theory of Action*, Academic Press, New York, 1982.

5. Talcott Parsons, *Structure and Process in Modern Societies*, Free Press, New York, 1960.

CHAPTER 4

1. Philip Zaleski, "The Flattened Cosmos," *Parabola*, Vol. 9, No. 1, January 1984, p. 82.

2. For example, according to Harland Cleveland, "the informatization of society will force dramatic changes in some long-standing hierarchic forms of social organization." This erosion of hierarchies by information technology challenges the rules, norms, and conventions that, in an earlier time, served to organize society by vesting economic and social power. Cleveland cites five hierarchies as bases for discrimination and unfairness; i.e., hierarchies of power based on control, hierarchies of influence based on secrecy, hierarchies of class based on ownership, hierarchies of privilege based on early access to valuable resources, and hierarchies of politics based on geography. See Harland Cleveland, "The Twilight of Hierarchy: Speculations on the 'Global Information Society,'" in *Information Technologies and Social Transformation*, Bruce R. Guile, ed., National Academy Press, Washington, D.C., 1985, pp. 55–80.

3. Donald A. Schön, *Beyond the Stable State*, W.W. Norton, New York, 1971.

4. Donna Lloyd-Kolkin, "Communication Network Analysis of an Educational Dissemination System: The Research and Development Exchange," Ph.D. dissertation, Stanford University, 1979.

5. Everett M. Rogers and Pi-Chao Chen, *Report of the Chinese Rural Health Systems Delegation*, National Academy of Sciences Committee on Scholarly Communication with the People's Republic of China, Washington, D.C., 1979.

6. James Legge, trans., *The Lî Kî*, Sacred Books of the East, Vol. 27, London, 1926, reprinted 1966.

7. Confucius, *Analects* 3:17, in Wing-tsit Chan, *A Source Book in Chinese Philosophy*, Princeton University Press, Princeton, 1963.

8. Vernon Boggs and William Kornblum, "Symbiosis in the City," *The Sciences*, January/February 1985, pp. 25–30.

9. Lisbeth Mark, *The Book of Hierarchies*, Quill Publisher, New York, 1984, p. 15.

10. Howard H. Pattee, *Hierarchy Theory: The Challenge of Complex Systems*, George Braziller, New York, 1973.

11. David K. Hurst, "Of Boxes, Bubbles and Effective Management," *Harvard Business Review*, May–June 1984, pp. 78–88.

12. Everett M. Rogers and D. Lawrence Kincaid, *Communication Networks: Toward a New Paradigm for Research*, Free Press, New York, 1981.

13. Typical comprehensive bibiliographies on social networks include:

Connections, the Bulletin of the International Network for Social Network Analysis (INSNA), is published triannually at the Centre for Urban and Community Studies at the University of Toronto. It includes brief summaries of applications of networks, surveys, and abstracts of research reports and publications in the field.

Linton C. Freeman, *A Bibliography of Social Networks,*, Monticello, Illinois, Council of Planning Librarians, Exchange Bibliography, 1976, pp. 1170–1171. Over 1,600 publications are cited.

Forest R. Pitts, "Bibliography: Recent Trends in Social Network Analysis," 1979. This paper was presented at the seminar on Communcation Network Analysis at the East-West Communication Institute in Honolulu. Over 481 items are listed.

14. Tim Heald, *Networks: Who We Know and How We Use Them*, Hodder and Stoughton, London, 1983, p. 13.

CHAPTER 5

1. Sir E. B. Tylor, *Primitive Culture*, J. Murray, London, 1871.

2. Elliott Jacques, *Project Health: The Pressure Principle*, G. D. Searle, Skokie, Ill., 1972, p. 12.

3. Peter S. Heller and Allan A. Tait, *Government Employment and Pay: Some International Comparisons*, IMF, Washington, D.C., 1984.

4. Noel McInnis, "Networking: A Way to Manage Our Changing World?", *Futurist*, Vol. 18, No. 3, June 1984, pp. 9–10.

5. Warren Bennis, "Beyond Bureaucracy," in *Sociological Realities: A Guide to the Study of Society*, Irving Louis Horowitz and Mary Symons Strung, eds., Harper and Row, New York, 1971, pp. 143–147.

6. Tim Heald, *Networks: Who We Know and How We Use Them*, Hodder and Stoughton, London, 1983.

7. Parker Rossman, "The Network Family," *Futurist*, December 1985, pp. 19–21.

8. Robert Custer and Harry Milt, *When Luck Runs Out: Help for Compulsive Gamblers and Their Families*, Facts on File Publications, New York, 1985.

9. Joshua Lederberg, "Network New York," *The Sciences*, December 1980, pp. 6–8.

10. Donald A. Schön, *Beyond the Stable State*, W.W. Norton, New York, 1971, p. 191

11. Ibid., p. 192

12. David Katz, "The Network Overlay: Helping Large Bureaucracies Do Things Better," *Bureaucrat*, Fall 1980, pp. 24–29.

13. Malcolm R. Parks, Charlotte M. Stan, Leona L. Essert, "Romantic Involvement and Social Network Involvement," *Social Psychology Quarterly*, Vol. 46, No. 2, June 1983, pp. 116–131.

14. Mary Scott Welch, *Networking: The Great Way for Women to Get Ahead*, Harcourt Brace Jovanovich, New York, 1980.

CHAPTER 6

1. Paul Barker, *The Guardian Weekly*, October 30, 1983.

2. Paul Dickson, *The Official Explanations*, Arrow Books, London, 1981, p. 171.

3. Martin L. Ernst, *Futurescope: Information Age Opportunities. Mapping the Evolution of Information Products and Services*, November 1983, pp. 1–48.

4. Network theory has numerous, and nowadays obvious, applications in communications, electrical circuitry, and economics. Its originator, Swiss

mathematician Leonhard Euler (1707–83), developed his investigation from two dimensions to three and devised a simple law for determining the predictable relationship in a polyhedron between its points, edges, and sides.

5. Bro Uttal, "The Best Software for Executives," *Fortune*, December 26, 1983, p. 156.

6. C. Jackson Grayson, Jr., "Networking by Computer," *Futurist*, June 1984, pp. 14–17.

CHAPTER 7

1. Ludwig von Bertalanffy, *Robots, Men and Minds*, George Braziller, New York, 1967.

2. Kurt Lewin, *A Dynamic Theory of Personality: Selected Papers*, McGraw-Hill, New York, 1935.

3. Erik Erikson, "Identity and the Life Cycle," *Psychological Issues*, Vol. 1, No. 1, 1959. Also see Charles Hampden-Turner, *Maps of the Mind*, Mitchell Beazley, London, 1981.

4. For those interested, see Johannes M. Pennings, *Interlocking Directorates*, Jossey–Bass, San Francisco, 1980; Mark S. Migruchi, *The American Corporate Network*, Sage Library of Social Research, Vol. 138, Sage Publications, Beverly Hills, Calif., 1982; Ronald S. Burt, "Cooptive Corporate Actor Networks," *Administrative Science Quarterly*, Vol. 25, No. 3, 1980.

Also see Ronald S. Burt, *Toward a Structural Theory of Action*, Academic Press, New York, 1982. On pages 325–326 Burt observes that while directorate ties facilitate transactions between establishments, they must at the same time inhibit transactions. Directorate ties bear a striking resemblance to the ceremonial necklaces and bracelets, *vaygu'a*, exchanged among natives in the primitive barter economy of the Trobriand Archipelago, as originally described by anthropologist Malinowski (1922). Similar to seats on a prestigious directorate, these ornaments are neither used nor regarded as money or currency, Each piece of *vaygu'a* has one main object throughout its existence—to be possessed and exchanged under prescribed conditions. The ceremonial exchange of necklaces and bracelets (or directorate seats) is accompanied by secondary activities. With the ritual exchange of arm-shells and necklaces, the natives carry on bartering from one island to another a number of utilities, often unprocurable in the district to which they are imported and indispensable there. Directors going through boardroom rituals carry on their network relationships within and outside of the role of being a director, operating from a position of perceived power and influence.

5. Ronald S. Burt, *Toward a Structural Theory of Action*; Everett M. Rogers and Rekha Agarwala-Rogers, *Communication in Organizations*, Free Press, New York, 1976.

6. For a more lucid exposition see Keith G. Provan, "The Federation as an Interorganizational Linkage Network," *Academy of Management Review*, Vol. 8, No. 1, 1983, pp. 79–89.

CHAPTER 8

1. K. M. Reese, "Newscripts," *Chemical Engineering News*, August 18, 1980, p. 64.

CHAPTER 9

1. "Patterns and Problems of Technological Innovation in American Industry," Report for the National Science Foundation, Washington, D.C., September 1963, PB 18 1573.

2. Robert K. Mueller, *The Innovation Ethic*, American Management Association, New York, 1971.

3. Mark Hanan, "Corporate Growth Through Venture Management," *Harvard Business Review*, January–February 1969.

4. *Management Perspectives on Innovation: Innovation Management Practices Among Companies in North America, Europe and Japan*, Arthur D. Little, Cambridge, Mass., 1985.

5. *From Vision to Reality: Successfully Managing Innovation*, Arthur D. Little, Cambridge, Mass., 1985.

CHAPTER 10

1. Byron Kennard, *Nothing Can Be Done, Everything Is Possible*, Brick House Publishing, Andover, Mass., 1982.

2. Hazel Henderson, *Creating Alternative Futures: The End of Economies*, Berkley Publishing, New York, 1978.

3. For a guide to community network building see *Building Networks: Cooperation as a Strategy for Success in a Changing World*, Norman T. Gilroy and Jim Swan, eds., Kendall–Hunt, Dubuque, Iowa, 1984.

4. Luther P. Gerlach and Virginia H. Hine, *People, Power, Change: Movements of Social Transformation*, Bobbs–Merrill, New York, 1970.

5. Virginia H. Hine, "The Basic Paradigm of a Future Socio-Cultural System," *World Issues*, April/May 1977.

6. Charles J. Fombrun, "Strategies for Network Research in Organizations," *Academy of Management Review*, Vol. 7, No. 2, 1982, pp. 280–291.

7. Tim Heald, *Networks: Who We Know and How We Use Them*, Hodder and Stoughton, London, 1983, p. 178.

8. Allen Parker and Marianne Hedin, "Networks in Education," *Forum*, March 1983, pp. 30–32.

9. Leif Smith and Patricia Wagner, *The Networking Game*, Network Resources, Denver, Colo., 1983.

APPENDIX

1. Robert K. Mueller, *Buzzwords: A Guide to the Language of Leadership*, Van Nostrand Reinhold, New York, 1974.

GLOSSARY

1. John A. Pearce II and Fred R. David, "A Social Network Approach to Organizational Design-Performance," *Academy of Management Review*, Vol. 8, No. 4, 1983, pp. 436–444.

2. Ibid.

3. Noel M. Tishy, Michael L. Tushman, and Charles Fombrun, "Social Network Analysis for Organizations," *Academy of Management Review*, Vol. 4, No. 4, 1979, pp. 507–519.

4. Pearce and David, "Social Network Approach."

5. Ralph H. Kilmann, "Coping with Social Complexity" *Human Systems Management*, Vol. 3, 1982, pp. 66–76; David Rubenstein and Richard W. Woodman, "Spiderman and the Burma Raiders: Collateral Organization Theory in Action," *Journal of Applied Behavioral Science*, Vol. 20, No. 1, 1984, pp. 1–21.

6. Pearce and David, "Social Network Approach."

7. Everett M. Rogers and Rekha Agarwala-Rogers, *Communication in Organizations*, Free Press, New York, 1976, p. 108.

8. Tishy, Tushman, and Fombrun, "Social Network Analysis."

9. J. R. Blau and Richard A. Alba, "Empowering Nets of Participation," *Administrative Science Quarterly*, Vol. 27, 1982, pp. 363–379.

10. Ronald S. Burt, *Toward a Structural Theory of Action*, Academic Press, New York, 1982, pp. 31–32.

11. Keith G. Provan, "The Federation as an Interorganizational Linkage Network," *The Academy of Management Review*, Vol. 8, No. 1, 1983, pp. 79–89.

12. Jessica Lipnack and Jeffrey Stamps, *Networking: The First Report and Directory*, Doubleday, New York, 1982, pp. 226–227; Jessica Lipnack and Jeffrey Stamps, "Discovering Networking" in *Networking: Theory and Practice*, Association for Humanistic Psychology, July 1983 (newsletter, special issue).

13. Rogers and Agarwala-Rogers, *Communication in Organizations*; Tishy, Tushman, and Fombrun, "Social Network Analysis."

14. Tony Gregore, "The Next Step Beyond Synergy," *Leading Edge Bulletin*, Vol. 3, No. 9, January 31, 1983, pp. 1–2.

15. Lisbeth Mark, *The Book of Hierarchies*, Quill Publisher, New York, 1984, p. 11.

16. Ibid.; Howard Pattee, *Hierarchy Theory: The Challenge of Complex Systems*, George Braziller, New York, 1973, pp. 4–6.

17. Gregore, "Next Step Beyond Synergy."

18. Pearce and David, "Social Network Approach."

19. Lipnack and Stamps, *Networking*; Lipnack and Stamps, "Discovering Networking."

20. Blau and Alba, "Empowering Nets of Participation."

21. Pearce and David, "Social Network Approach"; Tishy "Social Network Analysis."

22. Lipnack and Stamps, *Networking*; Lipnack and Stamps, "Discovering Networking."

23. Pearce and David, "A Social Network Approach"; Tishy, Tushman, and Fombrun, "Social Network Analysis."

24. Tishy, Tushman, and Fombrun, "Social Network Analysis."

25. Ibid.

26. Tim Heald, *Networks*, Hodder and Stoughton, London, 1983, p. 106.

27. Tishy, Tushman, and Fombrun, "Social Network Analysis."

28. Heald, *Networks.*

29. Lipnack and Stamps, *Networking*; Lipnack and Stamps, "Discovering Networking."

30. Tishy, Tushman, and Fombrun, "Social Network Analysis."

31. Burt, *Toward a Structural Theory.*

32. Tishy, Tushman, and Fombrun, "Social Network Analysis."

33. Ibid.

34. Karl E. Weick, *The Social Psychology of Organizing*, Addison-Wesley, Reading, Mass., 1979, pp. 3, 19, 20.

35. Ibid.

36. Luther P. Gerlach and Virginia H. Hine, *People, Power, Change: Movements of Social Transformation*, Bobbs–Merrill, New York, 1970, pp. 33–61.

37. Pearce and David, "Social Network Approach."

38. Miceal Ross, ed., *Operational Research: 1972 Proceedings of Sixth IFORS, Dublin, Ireland*, North Holland Publishing, Amsterdam.

39. Tishy, Tushman, and Fombrun, "Social Network Analysis."

40. Gregore, "Next Step Beyond Synergy."

41. J. C. Mitchell, ed., *Social Networks in Urban Situations*, University of Manchester Press, Manchester, England, 1969, p. 2.

42. Joseph Fiksel, "Dynamic Evolution in Social Networks," *Journal of Mathematical Sociology*, Vol. 7, 1980, p. 27.

43. Donald A. Schön, *Beyond the Stable State*, W.W. Norton, New York, 1971, p. 108.

44. Virginia Hine, "The Basic Paradigm of a Future Socio-Cultural System," *World Issues*, April/May 1977.

45. Pearce and David, "Social Network Approach."

46. Tishy, Tushman, and Fombrun, "Social Network Analysis."

47. Gregore, "Next Step Beyond Synergy."

48. Ibid.

49. Ibid.

50. Tishy, Tushman, and Fombrun, "Social Network Analysis."

51. Pearce and David, "Social Network Approach."

52. Lipnack and Stamps, *Networking*; Lipnack and Stamps, "Discovering Networking."

INDEX

Academic costumes, symbols of, 45–46
Action theory of networking, 35–37
Activist networks, 114
Ad hoc networks, 65
Adams, Robert M., 98
Agricultural research, 78–79
Agriculture, Department of, 43
Airline travel credits, 5–6
Alternative research centers, 92–93
Ambition-driven first initiative, 82, 85–86
Amdox, 75
American Council on Transplantation, 50
American Express, 9
American Telephone & Telegraph Company, 35, 75, 78, 97
Anet Paradox, 70
Ankara, Turkey, 19–20
Antiwar movements, 52
Apple Computers, 9, 68
Aquinas, St. Thomas, 41

Artificial intelligence applications, 33
ASEA (Allmänna Svenska Elektriska Aktiebolaget), 36, 104
Attribute networks, 49, 107–108, 113, 122
Australia, 55
Ayckbourn, Alan, 17–18

Bank of America, 9
Barker, Paul, 72
Barter, 53
Bavelas, A., 20
Belgium, 40, 55, 91
Bell, Daniel, 40
Bennis, Warren, 58
Bertalanffy, Ludwig von, 81
Bertram, Lavinia, 17
Beyond the Stable State (Schön), 64–65
Bhopal disaster, 12, 50
Bierce, Ambrose, 30

Black power movements, 52
Block model analysis, 116–117
Boardroom network, 39
Bolt Beranek and Newman, 97
Bottom-up idea generation approach, 104
Boundary-spanners, 72
Boutiques de sciences, 91
Brandeis, Louis, 86
British Civil Service, 55
British Petroleum, 42
Bureaucracy, 15, 16, 32, 40, 54–71
Burt, Ronald S., 35–37
BUSINESSnet, 76
Buzzwords, 129–131

Canada, 40, 55
Caracas community, 112
Carnegie Council on Children, 60
Centers, hi-touch, 89–94
Centrality, 126
Change-directed action, 82–83, 86
Chemical Estate Network, 10–13
Chemical industry, 10–13
Cheswick Center of Boston, 76–77, 89–90, 113, 125
"Cheswick Process, The: Seven Steps to a More Effective Board," 90
China, 28–29, 44
Church movements, 52
Citicorp, 36
Civil rights movements, 52
Civil service, 55
Cliques, 20, 46, 53, 82, 83, 86–87
Closed systems, 83–85
Club Méditerranée, 103
Code Napoleon, 63
Coleridge, Samuel Taylor, 33
Communication structures, 48–49
Communications Era Task Force, 79
Communications networks, 16, 72–79
Competition, 124, 125

Computer conferencing, 77
Computerese, 131
Comtel Information Systems, 75
Condition-driven choices, 83, 87
Conflict, 37, 40
Confucius, 44–45
Connectedness, 60, 61
Cooper, J. C., 14
Cooperative corporate actor networks, 86
Cosmopolites, 87
Council for Basic Education, 90
Countermovements, 111–112
Creating Alternative Futures (Henderson), 119
Credit unions, 6
Crime rates, 26
Critical paths, 110

Defense, Department of, 66–67
Defense Intelligence Agency, 66, 67
Denmark, 55
Density, 19
Dependence, 126
Director dyad, 86
Discipline, 24, 25
Dispersed networks, 60, 61
Diwanniyas, 28
Dow Chemical Company, 49–50, 97
Downey Side program, Springfield, Mass., 62
Dupont de Nemours, E. I., & Company, 36, 97

Economist, 39
Education, Department of, 43
Education, electronic, 75
E.G. & G., 97
Ego-identity, concept of, 82
Ego networks, 17, 19, 106–107, 113, 122, 123, 126
Electronic Information Exchange Systems (EIES), 77
Electronic mail, 76–77, 125

Electronics industry, 16
Elf Acquitaine, 36
Elitism, 52, 53, 125
Emerson, Ralph Waldo, 80, 82
Emerson Electric Company, 97
Employee clubs, 6
Employee discussion groups, 103
Environmental context, 85
Environmental movements, 52
Environmental Protection
    Agency, 43
Equitable Life Assurance Society, 69
Erikson, Erik, 82
"Establishment" groups, 52, 53

Family firms, 39, 40
Family hierarchies, 44, 46
Family networks, 15, 59–63
Family support networks, 60, 62
Favoritism, 112
Federal government, 10
Federation networks, 88
Federations, 39
Ferguson, Marilyn, 20
Field theory, 81
Fly-eyed networks, 21
Fombrun, Charles J., 122
Fortune magazine, 98
France, 91, 93
Futurist, The, 78

Gamblers Anonymous, 62
Gatekeepers, 72, 87, 123, 124
General Electric Company, 36, 104
Gerlach, Luther P., 20, 120
Giacco, Al, 42
Global interdependence, 112
Global market network manage-
    ment, 67–68
Goals, 126
Gossip, 74, 79, 85
GOVERNnet, 125
Grapevines, 5, 73–74, 79
Grass roots networks, 29–32

Grayson, C. Jackson, Jr., 77
Great Atlantic Radio Conspiracy,
    Baltimore, Maryland, 21
Great Britain, 29, 30–31, 55, 59, 69,
    91, 92–93
Grupo Manzana, 68
Guanxi, 28–29
Guys-who-really-know (GWRK)
    file, 7–8, 58

Hanan, Mark, 97
Harris, Irene, 69
Heald, Tim, 59, 69, 123
Health Services Administration, 43
Hedin, Marianne, 124
Henderson, Hazel, 20, 119
Hercules, Inc., 68
Herford, Robert, 17
Hierarchy, 1, 2, 15, 16, 21, 24–26,
    40, 57–58
    balancing networks with, 41–53
Highly connected networks, 60, 61
Hine, Virginia H., 20, 120
Holland, 91–94
Honeywell Information Systems, 78
Horizontal networks, 21, 42, 43–44
Hospice movement, 62
Human potential and response net-
    works, 50–52
Human-resource management,
    47–48
Human Systems Management Cir-
    cle, Fordham University, 127
Hurst, David K., 47
Hydra-headed networks, 21

IBM Corporation, 36, 75
ICI Inc., 36
Image, 111, 112
Incubation phase, 9, 100
Information exchange, 38
Information-knowledge spectrum,
    32–34
Information services, 16

Information technology, 73–79
Innovation Climate Index, 103
Innovation management, 95–105
Instinct, 36
Institute for the Information Society, 78
Institute for Liberty and Democracy, 31
Institute of Noetic Sciences, 64
Integration, 126
Intelligence, 66–67
Interlocking directorates, 39, 86
Internal Revenue Service, 32
International Institute for Applied Systems Analysis (IIASA), 54, 63
International Maize and Wheat Improvement Center, 79
International Monetary Fund, 55
International Network for Social Network Analysis, 127
International Rice Research, 79
Intimate Exchanges (Ayckbourn), 17–18
Introduction phase, 9, 100
Intuition, 35, 36
Invention phase, 9, 100
Islam, 62
Isolates, 86, 123, 124

Jackson, Jesse, 34
Jacques, Elliott, 55
Japan, 9, 26, 55, 99–103
Johnson, Samuel, 14
Jordan, W. Alec, 7–8
Jung, Carl, 47

Kay, Mary, 4
Kennard, Byron, 7, 119
Kenya, 27
Kinship networks, 15, 59, 112
Kissinger Associates, Inc., 117–118
Korea, Republic of, 48
Kristol, Irving, 49

Larsen, Judith, 16
Learned societies, 39, 52
Leavitt, H. J., 20
Levels, 21
Lewin, Kurt, 81, 82
Li, 44
Liaisons, 86, 87, 123
Lichtenberg, G. V. von, 95
Life space personality linkages, 81, 82
Linkages, 123
Linkers, 123, 124
Lipnack, Jessica, 15, 20, 21
Little, Arthur D., Inc., 6, 9–13, 25–26, 95, 96, 99, 102, 104, 113
Lobbying, 10
Local area networks, 75
Loosely organized systems (LOS), 14–15
Lundeen, Robert W., 50

Management control theory, 39
Management by objectives, 124
Manorial system, 63
Mark, Lisbeth, 46
Market networks, 67–68
Marquis, Don, 28
Mary Kay Cosmetics, Inc., 4
Massingberd Dynasties, 59
Maya of Zinacantan, 19
McDonald, Tracy M., 56
McInnis, Noel, 55
Medtronic, 9, 104
Membership associations, 37, 39
Merrill Lynch Pierce Fenner & Smith, Inc., 9, 36
Metanetworks, 78
Metasystems Design Group, Arlington, Virginia, 78
Microcomputer Information Support Tools (MIST), 78
Mid-management dyad, 86
Monopoly, 112
Monsanto Company, 68
Mutual support, 28

Nairobi, Kenya, 27
National Association of Corporate Directors, 87
National Association for Female Executives, 70
National Diffusion Networks, 43
National Science Foundation, 35, 43, 95
"Network" (Great Britain), 69
Network analysis, 48–49
Network Builders International (NBI), 22
"Network New York" model, 63, 64
Network roles, 65–66
Networking: The First Report and Directory, 59
Networking Institute, West Newton, Mass., 78
Networkmanship, 112–118
Networks (Heald), 59, 69
"Networks" (New York), 69–70
Networks and networking
  action theory, 35–37
  activist, 114
  ad hoc, 65
  adaptive magic of, 57–59
  attribute, 49, 107–108, 113, 122
  balancing with hierarchy, 41–53
  vs. bureaucracy, 55–57
  centers, 89–94
  characteristics of, 116–117
  chemical industry and, 10–13
  communications, 16, 72–79
  concepts, 115–116
  defined, 14–15, 129–130
  designing and setting up, 119–127
  ego, 17, 19, 106–107, 113, 122, 123, 126
  family, 15, 59–63
  grass roots, 29–32
  guys-who-really-know (GWRK) file, 7–8, 58
  horizontal, 21, 42, 43–44
  information-knowledge spectrum, 32–34
  kinship, 15, 59, 112
  managing innovative, 95–105
  market, 67–68
  nature of, 2–6, 20–22
  nourishing, 6–7
  old boy, 39, 52, 59, 69, 107, 111
  organization, 25–26
  overlays, 66–67
  personal obligation, 19
  positional, 17, 19, 20, 49, 108, 113, 122, 123
  processes, 22
  professional, 24–25
  purposes of, 10
  romantic, 68–69
  scientific, 63–64
  search for new social geometry, 81–88
  shadow, 64–66
  sociai, 36–40, 47–53, 109
  social order and, 26–27
  structures, 21
  support, 60, 62, 108, 109
  technology, 92–93
  transactional, 107, 113, 122
  tribal, 15–16, 111
  uses of, 117
  vertical vs. horizontal, 21, 42–44
  women's, 69–70
Networkspeak, 129–131
New girl networks, 69
New York Academy of Medicine, 64
New York Academy of Sciences, 64
New Zealand, 55
Nomadism, 103
Novak, Alma, 69
Nuclear family, 59, 60

Office automation, 73–75
Old boy networks, 39, 52, 59, 69, 107, 111
OMNET, Inc., 76
Operations research theory, 110
Opinion Research Corporation, 99
Order of Maria Theresa, 34

Organic-adaptive structure, 58
Organizational change, 80–81
Organizational theory, 37
Organized labor unions, 46
Overlay networks, 66–67

Page, Karen A., 56
Palestinians, 62
Parker, Allen, 124
Parsons, Talcott, 37
Participate, 77
Partnerships, 38, 39
Patron clientelism, 112
Pei, Mario Andrew, 131
Personal networks: see Ego net-
    works
Personal obligation networks, 19
Pert charts, 110
Peru, 31–32
Phase changes, 33
Piaget, Jean, 32
Poincaré, Raymond, 95
Poland, 62–63
Position centrality model, 20
Position prestige model, 20
Positional networks, 17, 19, 20, 49,
    108, 113, 122, 123
Postal Service, 43
Power, 10, 23–24, 39
Power groups, 53
Primitive societies, 15
Productivity circles, 103
Professional networking, 24–25
Professional organizations, 40,
    46, 52
Promotion, 24
Proprietorships, 38

Quality circles, 103

Raiffa, Howard, 54, 71
Record of Ritual, The, 44
Reese, K. M., 89
Regional Medical Program, 43

Religious movements, 111
Reticulist, 14
Rewards, 101–102
Rockefeller University, 63
Rogers, Everett M., 16, 48–49
Romantic networks, 68–69
Rosett, Claudia, 31, 32
Royal relationships, 111
Rumor mills, 5
Russelsteel, Inc., 47

Sarason, Seymour B., 7, 127
Satellite links, 64
Saudi Arabia, 28
Schlage Electronics, Inc., 9
Schön, Donald, 43, 64–65
Science magazine, 93
Science shops, 91–93
SCIENCEnet, 76
Scientific networks, 63–64
Scientific thinking, 41–42
Self-actualization, 42
Self-help, concept of, 29–32
Severed networks, 107–108
Shadow networks, 64–66
Shakespeare, William, 53
Sharish, 62
Shaw, George Bernard, 104
Sierra Club, 33
Silicon Valley, 16
Silicon Valley Fever (Rogers and
    Larsen), 16
Smith, Leif, 8, 126
Social aggregations, 23
Social class hegemony theory, 39
Social clubs, 46
Social context, 85
Social contracts, hidden, 23, 27
Social entrepreneur movement, 29,
    30–31
Social events, 3–4, 6–7
Social networks, 36–40, 47–53, 109
Social order, networks and, 26–27
Social reform organizations, 52

Social systems theory, 37
Social traps, 51–52
Socialization, 35, 36
Society for the Advancement of
    General Systems, 81
Soixantehuitards, 93
Source, The, 77
Soviet Communist party, 26
Spiderweb network, 56
SP(I)N [segmented, polycephalous
    (ideological) network], 120
Sports events, 6
Spurgeon, Charles Haddon, 105
Stamps, Jeffrey, 15, 20, 21
Stars, 123, 124
Street people, 45
Stress, adaptation to, 37
Subcultures (platforms), 49
Sumitomo Chemical Company,
    36, 68
Support networks, 60, 62, 108, 109
Sweden, 55
Systems view of hierarchies, 46–47
Sytek, 75

TACHAI Brigade, Shensi Province,
    China, 44
Tandem Computer, Inc., 3–4
Technological innovations, 51
Technology networks, 92–93
Teleconferencing, 77
TeleLearning Systems, 75
TELEnet, 125
Teletraining, 78
3M Company, 9, 36, 97, 98
3M Technical Forum, 98
Tightly organized systems (TOS), 15
Times Square, New York, 45
Tolkatch, 65
Tomalin, Nicholas, 52
Top-down communication, 42–43
Top management dyad, 86
Top management view of innovation
    process, 99–102

Transactional networks, 107, 113,
    122
Transfer points, 92
Transformational networks, 79
Transnational Network for
    Appropriate/Alternative Tech
    nologies (TRANET), 78
Transplantation, 50
Transportation, Department of, 43
Transportation systems, 16
Travelers Insurance Company, 78
Trendsetters, 72
Treybig, Jim, 3
Tribal networks, 15–16, 111
Trust, 30, 47, 124
TRW Company, 103
Turkey, 19–20, 26
TWG energy Field, 79
Tylor, Sir E. B., 54

Underarchy (worker) dyad, 86
Underhill, Pat, 70
Union Carbide Corporation, 12
Union of Soviet Socialist Republics
    (USSR), 63–64, 65
U.S. Radio, Inc., 78
Universities, 52
Urban blight crisis, 29
Urban innovation networking,
    43–44
Uttal, Bro, 75

Venture organizational concept,
    97–98
Vertical networks, 21, 42–43
Violent Criminal Apprehension
    Program (VKAP), 75–76

Wagner, Patricia, 8, 126
Wallenda, Karl, 35
Wallenda family, 35
Wang Laboratories, Inc., 75
Watzlawick, P., 34
Weapon system development, 96

Weavers, 8, 123, 124
Weblike structure, 55–56
Weick, K. S., 15
Weizsäcker, C. F. von, 32
Welch, Mary Scott, 69
West Germany, 55
Westinghouse Monsanto, 97
Wetenschapswinkels, 91–94
Wholeparts, 21

"Wicker" project, Sheffield, England, 31
Women's networks, 69–70

Xerox Corporation, 75

Young Women's Forum of New York, 56–57

Zaleski, Philip, 41